Education's Missing Ingredient

What Parents Can Tell Educators

Victoria M. Young

ROWMAN & LITTLEFIELD EDUCATION
A division of

Rowman & Littlefield Publishers, Inc.
Lanham • New York • Toronto • Plymouth, UK

Published by Rowman & Littlefield Education
A division of Rowman & Littlefield Publishers, Inc.
A wholly owned subsidiary of The Rowman & Littlefield Publishing Group, Inc.
4501 Forbes Boulevard, Suite 200, Lanham, Maryland 20706
http://www.rowmaneducation.com

Estover Road, Plymouth PL6 7PY, United Kingdom

British Library Cataloguing in Publication Information Available

Library of Congress Cataloging-in-Publication Data

Young, Victoria M., 1956–
  Education's missing ingredient : what parents can tell educators / Victoria M. Young.
    p. cm.
  Includes bibliographical references.
  ISBN 978-1-60709-346-6 (cloth : alk. paper) — ISBN 978-1-60709-347-3
  (pbk. : alk. paper) — ISBN 978-1-60709-348-0 (electronic)
  1. Public schools—United States. 2. Education—Aims and objectives—United States. 3.
Education—Parent participation—United States. I. Title.
  LA217.2Y68 2009
  370.73—dc22   2009021857

Printed in the United States of America

  ∞ ™ The paper used in this publication meets the minimum requirements of American
National Standard for Information Sciences—Permanence of Paper for Printed Library
Materials, ANSI/NISO Z39.48-1992. Printed in the United States of America

This book is dedicated to my mother,

Adeline Magnotta Young,

and all those like her

who take the time to listen.

No law or ordinance is mightier than understanding.

Plato

TABLE OF CONTENTS

PREFACE

If parents "do not understand," is it not, in part at least, because educators have been woefully negligent about seriously "educating" parents about classrooms, schools, roles, pressures, constraints?

Seymour B. Sarason

As a parent, in addition to giving my unconditional love and support to my children, three major responsibilities are mine to bear. Those obligations are to keep my children healthy, keep them safe, and provide them with the best education possible. As a parent seeking quality in education, I have failed.

Making sure our children were rested, well fed, and respectful of others was not enough. Reading to them almost every night starting when they were very young, being involved in the classroom, participating in our parent teacher organization, keeping myself informed as much as possible about educational issues, and even going to school board meetings was not enough. I did everything I knew, at the time, to try to ensure the best opportunity for a good education for our children. I trusted the education professionals to do the rest. I trusted the schools.

My trust turned out to be misplaced. That trust is forever gone but I am still optimistic that true, lasting improvement can occur in the public education system of the United States, and it must. When *Nation at Risk* was published in 1983, that was supposed to be a defining moment when the lights would go on in the minds of all Americans and the importance of and need to improve education in every classroom in the United States would be illuminated.

The reality is that too few people grasp the current situation and understand the consequences a poor education system can have on a country. People aren't realizing education's influence on their top concerns: the economy, health care, and climate change. Others say, "If it's not broken, don't fix it." But at what point do we admit the education system is broken? Is it when workers can't fill out an application or make correct change or when the quality and essential quantity of our college and university personnel declines to an irreversible level?

Historically, there would have been no need for true equal educational opportunity in the United States if we were going to maintain a slave class. If our educational goal in the United States now is to maintain a subservient lower class, then don't change our system. If you feel satisfied with the idea that educational opportunity is for the "haves" and mediocrity in education is fine for the "have-nots," then let us do nothing but stage reforms that benefit a few and give some well-meaning people a warm fuzzy feeling while the majority of our children, and our country, gets left behind in this now-global economy that we have created. Every day we are losing American talent that we don't even know exists; it is talent that is unrecognizable in the disinterested students being viewed as hopeless.

Who am I to be speaking about education? I am the daughter of a teacher who was fortunate enough to have earned his college education through the World War II GI Bill combined with income from our local iron factory, which no longer exists. He came from a large family whose father died young, leaving his mother to take in laundry to "make ends meet." My dad not only taught mathematics for thirty years but also built his own little empire of small businesses in our town. He lives the American Dream. Education provided him that opportunity. And in turn, I was fortunate that he stressed to our family and modeled for us the importance of hard work and education.

I am just a parent who sees herself as an ordinary American who was educated in the K–12 public education system and has navigated my own two children through it. I am a common, middle-class person who worked hard to invest in my own education with help from my family and loans. The belief was that education would serve as a safety net for remaining in the middle class; it would keep me out of poverty. It was an investment that has served me well.

My own paths in education led me to choose the much respected profession of veterinary medicine. Having practiced veterinary medicine for twenty-two years and having been actively involved in education as a parent for eighteen years, the correlations between my profession and teaching are profoundly remarkable. Like practicing veterinary medicine, the practice of teaching is both an art and a science. I hope the reader does not take offense at the comparison of teaching children to training and working with animals, for none is intended.

Within the traditional public school system, I am just a parent. Most would not consider me to be your average parent; I was more directly involved in the schools than the average parent. Being a parent in the educational realm implies that you have no credentials in the field of education. That is a fact in my case.

Now, consider that much of my time in veterinary medicine was spent on farms or in exam rooms communicating with everyday people about problems, solutions, and prevention of problems. Those processes in veterinary medicine I understand well. Those are the same processes that should be applied to the problems of our education system. Gaining insight into these issues through the education system's "school of hard knocks" gives a person a unique perspective of the solutions.

Please don't close your ears and minds to me because I lack educational credentials. Find the patience and respect to listen and consider my views because I am one parent who has behaved like the scientist within me. I have observed children learning, teachers teaching, administrators doing their thing, and the actions of our school board along with some interaction with state and federal educational bureaucracies. I noted my observations, unconsciously at first and mainly mentally but sometimes in notes to myself or editorials in the newspaper. I reviewed, researched, and evaluated my beliefs against many others in the education field, both current and historical. I listened to others and reflected.

In the end, it seems we need to base development of a teaching philosophy on our beliefs and principles, observed correlations, knowledge of the developing brain, and common sense. We must become and remain vigilant to the constantly changing needs of our communities and the educational structures that are of integral importance to building and maintaining successful communities. Our goals must be based on the desires and needs of our people.

That is the combination of thoughts that leads to the one idea presented within this book that is mine and stems from my belief that the largest single problem with the so-called education system of the United States is its failure to listen to the people it was supposed to serve. My hope is to contribute to the development of a deeper understanding of this concept and its role in providing the solutions to the struggles occurring within our failing schools and our failing United States public education system.

The ideas, suggestions, and solutions in this book are mainly taken from others. There are many in the past and the present that have the answers to improving the K–12 American education system. They fuel my optimism and drive my desire to make their voices heard. In attempting to do that, I found myself using clichés and quoting others; neither of these would I normally do. So, I ask the reader not to think of the well-known phrases as clichés but rather to think of them as wise thoughts from the past that have been repeated so often they have become clichés. I ask the reader to hear those words anew as voices from the past trying to echo words of wisdom to us.

The major resolving principles and beliefs contained in this book correlate not only with the historical beliefs of many but with modern research. This is not to insinuate that this book is research-based in the strict sense of the words. Rather, it should more appropriately be considered experience-based and research-backed, since much of what I found in my research over the years goes unnoted because I was reading for interest and not with the intent of writing a book. I could not now go back and track all the input that went into my decision making.

Remember, my beliefs, from the perspective of a parent, were based first on observation and common sense about how children learn. But, when common sense and research do align, shouldn't we give those concepts our focused attention? To thoughtfully consider the current needs of our education system, we have to begin with understanding. If you have personally had no problems, then the education system failures are more difficult for you to conceptualize; you do have to identify and understand a problem before you can resolve it.

For me, this issue is no longer personal. This book is not written to share the minute details of my often turbulent experiences. You can find books about horror stories that have occurred in some schools; this is not one of those books. Brief, true stories are used in the first few chapters and occasionally throughout to set the stage for understanding for those of you who have not experienced difficulties in the public education system. After all, most kids that make it through the public schools do so without any apparent problems. Many parents are aware of problems with public education but not in their school or with their child. Others are unaware of problems or don't associate their children's failures or societal problems with education. But is not the true test of education found in how we live life itself?

Many, undoubtedly, are able to fill in their own stories to illustrate my points. These are people that weren't so lucky in the great gamble for the best education for their children. I many times heard myself asking "Why me?" as I once again phoned or visited our school district's office. One has to consider walking away from the whole mess. Time and again you hear "you can't change the system"; "forgive and forget." Nearing the end of my own kids' time in the public schools, I wanted to forgive and forget the injustices I've seen and experienced in this "failing" school system. The problem is I feel the need to share what I've learned in hopes of improving the educational experience for others. To do that, there are things that should not be forgotten.

It would seem to be common sense to learn from our mistakes. We can't do that if we continue to walk away once our own children are done with school. Having just finished learning firsthand the lessons offered by being part of a failing system, parents and educators shouldn't forget and leave the next generation to experience the same problems. We know what mistakes have been made. But will anyone listen?

Our local school district provides a learning experience that culminates at its one high school containing 1,600-plus students, where the majority of students (approximately 52 percent) are Hispanic and the free and reduced lunch students currently make up about 60 percent which knows no racial lines. Elementary schools in the district vary in their demographics, with numbers in these same categories around 80 percent for some. The school demographics bring some unique problems to solve but the major problems are the same as for any other schools (urban, suburban, or rural), where maintaining a disciplined yet stimulating learning environment, quality educators and administration, and financial and community support in order to provide quality learning opportunities for all is the universal dilemma.

In reading the works of others, I was led to believe that the roots of these problems are also universal. One wrote about school boards and I wondered how I missed seeing him at mine; it sounded like our local board. Another wrote about her children in a public elementary school; it sounded like she was in our classrooms, but I never saw her either. Our stories are the same. The problems are manifested in classrooms all over, not just in "failed" schools. You find children having negative learning experiences almost everywhere; it's just a matter of degree, a matter of numbers. But the encouraging thing is that we do have the answers to our problems, with each school and each classroom having its own unique solutions. At this time, it is so very important that people understand their role in these solutions and the need for complete and thorough change.

Everywhere I go, I find that the common people instinctively know that change must occur soon. They sense that this country is in trouble. They feel it in their everyday lives. They are the reason that the current political buzz word is "change," but specific changes in education are not part of the talk. They should be. Granted, education is not a welcomed topic at cocktail parties but concrete educational issues should be talked about in the news, in the boardrooms, on the streets, in the coffee shops, and definitely should have merited more than one question in our latest presidential debates. We must agree that we, U.S. citizens, can do a better job educating all our citizenry than what we are currently doing.

As a country, we all have a stake in education. A government report in 1939 called *The Evaluation of Secondary Schools* summed up the situation well by stating, "In a democracy, a school should not be satisfied with being good; it should strive constantly to become better" (Cooperative Study of Secondary School Standards, 61).

The current reality is that too many people aren't at liberty to talk or don't want to talk about education. The views of parents, teachers, and students must be voiced, must be listened to, noted, and acted on; they shouldn't be rejected as just complaints. We shouldn't decide who to listen to based on their title, social standing, political clout, or any other discriminatory factor including the way they look or laugh. In a country founded on democratic ideals, we must constantly work at not making judgments without a fair hearing from the people. To keep our heads above water, to strive to stay one stroke ahead, we must act now to correct the mistakes of the past and prevent those in the future as best we can.

Our K–12 education system in the United States of America does not take the honor of being best in the world; it's not even second best. It is well below that using any measure. And being part of the public schools, at this moment in time, has left me feeling like I've fallen into a swiftly moving current, grasping at times for a hand-hold, but each time finding it out of reach. Living in a state traversed with treacherous white-water rivers and dangerous irrigation ditches, I warned my children repeatedly as they were growing up that if they fell into rapidly moving water: "Don't fight the current. Don't look back. Go with the flow and look for your chance to grab onto something to help you get out."

In some ways, life is like that swiftly moving stream. But it isn't identical. In life, we should look both forward and back. We must look back to learn from the mistakes and successes of the past yet always keep looking to the future with the hope of reaching our goals, fulfilling a vision. And there are times we must fight against the current.

Observation, research, and much trial and failure did produce in me a vision for the education system of the United States. That became agonizing, for sending your own children to school daily while recognizing and realizing what serious mistakes are being made is pure hell. On a regular basis, I wished I didn't know what I know; I wished I didn't care about the children, parents, and teachers suffering within this system. Facing the facts is hard to do.

Dare You Face Facts? by Muriel Lester served as my final inspiration to write about education. Through her book, she was appealing to the United States to lead Europe to peace, a peace based on mutual understanding with the help and unity of the spiritual and governmental leaders of America, a country in which she believed that "No other people has such initiative, such resourcefulness" (1940, 121). My interpretation of her drive to write that book was that she felt that knowing firsthand "about the happenings" in Europe, in China, and in Africa in the 1930s and 1940s left her "shouldering the burden of caring." She was reaching out with the hope of finding others who would care and hoped to move them to act. Like her, I feel that knowing what I know, and caring, in my case about the public education system of the United States, has been my burden.

Thinking about the times she must have gone through, my anguish and frustration can't compare. That thought gives me the energy to once more re-live my journey down the public education stream as just a parent who cares.

ACKNOWLEDGMENTS

Thank you to the National Science Resource Center for allowing use of their Theory of Action Model and for their contributions to science education. Their efforts to instruct teachers will reach beyond those borders, as they should.

Many people are represented among the thoughts and between the lines of this book. Some have been near and dear to me while others were strangers passing the time while waiting in lines, traveling on airplanes, or in the Laundromat. As you read, many of you will recall hearing some familiar words; I thank you for listening.

My local library provided the access to the books necessary to make this writing possible. Thank you, ladies, for always being helpful without ever knowing what you were helping accomplish—just doing your jobs. Thanks for being good at it.

Special thanks to my publishers, Rowman & Littlefield, for giving an unknown, uncredentialed, obscure individual a voice. And thank you to Patricia Stevenson for her patient and reassuring manner during the editing process. Particular thanks to Tom Koerner for setting the stage for my final revision by reminding me of my former English teachers, who seemed to be looking over my shoulder as I worked. Thanks to those teachers.

Sincere appreciation goes out to a teacher I have yet to personally meet, Dr. Seymour Sarason. He provided a seed for growth with his encouragement early in this endeavor. With what few words we exchanged, he made me believe I have something to say worth being said. His gentle goading made me question myself further and give more to my writing than I had originally anticipated, that being in keeping with what a true teacher does.

This book was enhanced through the efforts of Gina Ferguson, my former neighbor, fellow parent, and friend. Before knowing of the existence of this project, she was providing encouragement by sharing books, and her insight and experiences both of schools and life. She kept my feet to the fire at a crucial time and kept me in line with her uncanny ability to spot my human moments of laziness in my writing. From her timely enlightenment to her careful reading and questioning, she brought this book from a wish to a reality.

And we give recognition to her husband, Gary, and mine, Patrick—the men that stand behind us women but who themselves are strong parents and supporters for their children and their wives. And further acknowledgement goes to Gary and Gina's boys for unwittingly acting as little reminders as to why this effort is worthwhile.

To my own children, who will be reading this book for the first time along with the rest of you, words can't do justice. I sheltered you from the rough seas of my writing experience but it truly would not have come to being without you. I thank you both for the encouragement you unknowingly gave me through your support of my efforts to "stick-up for kids" all these years. I learn so much both from you and through you. Through the sometimes turbulent waters we travel, because of you two, the journey is always amazing. Thanks for teaching me through your eyes. I hope I set a good example and will now humbly except your critique as we once again travel down this stream together.

SAFE AND DISCIPLINED SCHOOLS

Government should actively promote good as well as repress evil. That is a free government where the people make their own laws; and that will be a good one where the people are wise and virtuous. But, virtue and wisdom do not come by inheritance; they must be propagated by education.

William Penn

Safe Schools

Sending your first child off to kindergarten is a very memorable moment. Living about six blocks from our elementary school, it was definitely within walking distance but it was at a point in time when parents were questioning the safety of children everywhere. The memory of a twelve-year-old boy being abducted while biking with his brother in rural Minnesota was all too fresh in our minds. So we decided to have our child ride the school bus. A bus stop was located one block away.

In a then-current parenting magazine, it was being suggested that if you were concerned about how your child might handle the bus ride to school and going on his or her way without you, you should find a spot at school where you can see him or her get off the bus but where they couldn't necessarily see you watching. For a first-timer looking for peace of mind, it sounded like a good idea.

1

CHAPTER 1

After seeing our son onto the bus, I hopped in the car and went over to the area where I knew kindergarteners would be gathering. From a distance, I saw him get off the bus and be directed around to the playground area. Shortly thereafter, he appeared in the area where kindergarten students were supposed to wait. Great! What a relief.

Unfortunately, that relief was short-lived. It began to dawn on me that from where I was standing I was looking out over a group of kindergarteners and first graders with no adult in sight. This area was around the side of the building so it was out of sight of the main playground. I was standing by a fence that only partially enclosed the area; it was open to the street. Surely, I must be mistaken. I looked and looked for that potentially really short adult. Waiting until the teachers came out to bring in the kids, the bell rang, and they were safely inside, I left for home and the telephone.

According to the school staff, they didn't have the playground duty schedule completed. My assumption at the time was that they took my comments to heart, about the area being open to the street and potentially dangerous in various ways, and were giving the resolution of this matter immediate attention. The next day, we repeated the pattern of the first day and once again that area was not supervised. Again, the school staff gave their assurance that they were working on the problem. The third day, same thing, only this time the complaint was left until the following morning.

That morning at the bus stop, I asked another mother if she was aware that no supervision was provided near the area open to the street. She was not. She also had a kindergartener and wanted to see for herself if it was a problem. She joined me at the spot where, once again, no adult was in sight. She was mad. And she had something that was apparently effective in changing the situation. She was tall, robust, and vocal in a commanding sort of way. It could have been a coincidence, but the next day adequate supervision was apparent.

Eighteen years have passed. I can't say for sure that proper supervision in that area continued. What is known is that the physical condition of the area, which makes it a safety issue, still exists and is recognized by others including the administration. It is clearly noted in a recent school district facilities report. You would think someone would have put up a secure fence by now.

Of course, being just parents, our views are often taken as being based more on sentimentality than substance. Or the administration may treat a problem as though it was the only time that particular problem has been brought to their attention and you, of course, are the only one having the problem; if only that were always true. Anecdotal is the word I've most often heard school administrators use to refer to parents' stories. It means they view this type of testimony as "entertaining accounts of some single happening" (*Webster's*, 1976). It implies that our stories are not necessarily fully truthful. They usually aren't confirmed by statistics; they many times can't be proved or disproved. Apparently, that justifies inaction even on what would appear to be a commonsense issue, like proper fencing.

Disciplined Schools

Three years after the fence incident, our second child entered kindergarten (different school, same district). The grounds were exceptional. It felt very safe. She loved going to school. All was wonderful until about two months into the school year when she got slammed from behind onto the blacktop. It was the result of standing in line waiting to go to music in a different building. She didn't have a scratch on her hands. She took it totally on the face. The unruly boy's father did call to somewhat apologize by saying "Boys will be boys."

The disciplinary consequences of this boy's action were never revealed to us by the school, leaving us to assume none occurred. At that point, we took a deep breath, didn't pursue the matter any further, and watched as our daughter suffered some major discomfort. Fortunately, time does heal wounds and she only has some minor scarring. This same boy, however, persisted in being a major disturbance to every one of the classrooms he shared with our daughter.

But he was of minor consequence compared to the boy labeled as "severely emotionally disturbed" who moved into this school and our daughter's classroom in the third grade. As a classroom volunteer it was obvious, through conversations with this new boy, that he was very smart and seemed to know right from wrong. He was very likeable. He was never a problem when I or anyone from the education department was in the room. But the reports from our daughter, confirmed by the teacher, were that he was being really destructive to school property, and disrespectful to the teacher and the assistant who had been assigned to supervise him.

This boy was disrupting the whole class. Upon asking the teacher if she had a problem with my going over her head to address this issue with the administration, her response was "Please do." That was the defining moment when the unconscious decision on my part was made to take on what would become a battle for safe and disciplined schools in our district.

Before anything was done to correct the disruptions in this classroom, this boy hit the teacher. That did not get him kicked out of school. It only got him into the detention room the next morning where he hit that supervisor, and that finally got him placed in a special program in a neighboring city. It could have been better for him if he had been handled differently. He was smart and needed expert help—help that he didn't get in this public school system. Unfortunately for the teacher and the other students in the class, the year was almost over when he was removed.

Safe and Disciplined Schools Issues

During this conflict, the decision to address the administration meant looking at our district policies, procedures, and state laws concerning discipline. In the course of these developments, various discussions occurred with the administration at all local levels. It appeared that policies were in place that could have helped before this classroom situation had escalated. Wasted instructional time could have been saved. The students' and teacher's year could have been much different. Obviously, misunderstandings had occurred.

In Idaho, we have a law that establishes the basic assumptions that govern the agreement to provide a thorough system of public schools, much the same as most states. In Idaho Code 33-1612, the first three of these assumptions deal with safe and disciplined school issues. The wise writers of this law may very well have put safe and disciplined school issues at the beginning of their list of assumptions to signify their importance to any further educational goals being realized. They are: "1) a safe environment conducive to learning is provided, 2) educators are empowered to maintain classroom discipline, and 3) the basic values of honesty, self-discipline, unselfishness, respect for authority, and the central importance of work are emphasized."

During this period of research and discovery, it became obvious through discussions with teachers that many didn't feel they were empowered to maintain discipline. In this law, it clearly states that they are empowered. Empowered means they are "permitted to, authorized, enabled, or given authority" (*Webster's*, 1976). Yet somehow we had gotten to the point where either we didn't understand the concept of discipline, we no longer were teaching teachers how to maintain discipline, or the teachers weren't getting the administrative, legal, or parental support to maintain discipline, or a combination thereof.

Feeling so strongly that we must get to the bottom of this issue, attending Safe and Drug-Free Schools Advisory Subcommittee and District Committee meetings were the next logical step to seeing what approach our district was taking. These committees had been required of our district as part of the settlement of a lawsuit. Their discussions seemed to point to the need for consistent procedures for discipline, on a district-wide basis.

After a December 17, 1998, meeting, the following was recorded: "Considerable discussion took place related to the importance of appropriate levels of continuity between buildings (middle to junior high to high school) relating to school rules, consequences, and procedures." It was decided that, through handbook revisions, this issue be addressed by building administration. This is how our system intended to fix itself.

Between December 1998 and April 1999, the situation was escalating in our daughter's classroom and other ongoing safety and discipline issues had surfaced in this school and other schools in the district. A small group of parents was growing impatient with the ongoing meetings and discussions and felt that the administration was only seeking input from a very limited, select group of patrons. It was decided that the best thing to do would be to call a town-hall type meeting to open the lines of discussion with more parents. The plan was to collect a wide variety of opinions on the issue of discipline and present a written summary to the school board that would include written anonymous comments to be collected after the meeting. The date of the meeting was set for April 20.

Before the meeting, issues were discussed with each principal, all of whom seemed to be very receptive to the proposal of an open exchange of ideas. Some of their comments were used anonymously on the overheads that were prepared as talking points for the evening. The answers to our school's discipline problems had not been predetermined by this group as evident by the question marks that surrounded the solutions section. The overheads looked like this:

Mutual Goals:
Ensure that no student prevents a teacher from doing his/her job
Ensure that our students' right to learn is not interfered with
Ensure a safe place to learn and work
Our Needs:
Establish respect
Establish consistency in policy and its implementation
Establish enforceable consequences that are enforced
?????????Solutions???????????:
District discipline policy that is consistent from building to
building
Social skills curriculum
Clear and concise parent and student information
Clear and concise teacher instruction
Safety devices
Keep It Simple
Respect, Consequences, Consistent
Discipline is the process of training a child so that the desired
character traits and habits can be developed.

On April 20, 1999, the meeting took place as scheduled. The next morning, the *Idaho Press Tribune* (our local paper) wrote that the meeting had been called by parents to discuss discipline and described how parents, school staff, and students filed into the meeting room still "reeling from news of the carnage in a Colorado high school."

For those of you who have forgotten, April 20, 1999, was the day the school shootings occurred at Columbine High School. It set a somber, respectful tone for the meeting. The shootings were of course mentioned by the participants, but all comments were very thoughtful and filled with concern rather than misplaced emotion. Later, this gathering was viewed by some as reactionary to the Columbine shootings.

On May 3, a composite of the opinions and ideas collected that night was sent to our school board and district administration along with a letter informing them that this issue would be presented at their May 10 board meeting. They were asked to consider one of the anonymous written suggestions submitted that night. That suggestion was the idea of setting up a task force to fully explore all questions, comments, and recommendations that were expressed by the attendees of the town hall meeting.

On May 7, a letter came from the superintendent stating that, after thinking about the comments, they had moved forward administratively "to provide a forum and relief for the concerns expressed that night." They believed that this existing structure was an "effective mechanism for dialogue and action surrounding the issues of school safety and discipline." In addition to the committees dictated by the existing disciplinary discrimination lawsuit, committees would also be set up in the elementary schools. The meetings would be monthly and were supposed to be designed to "meet the collective needs of our students and parents." Nice wording and that was where I was told to go!

But written anonymous comments had been collected that night and compiled in a booklet and, as promised, they were presented to the school board on May 10. The idea of the school board sanctioning a task force was clearly indicated in the document. It was not a new idea. The same idea had actually been written up in our state's *Safe and Disciplined Schools Resource Handbook* published in 1996. That handbook had outlined who should be on a task force and what processes they should go through for evaluation of conditions and gave sample agendas and ideas for identifying program elements.

As expressed to the school board and outlined for the community in an editorial, the "task" would be to sort through the recommendations and concerns that had been voiced on April 20 and to identify our school and community strengths, challenges, and limitations. The goal would be to come up with opportunities and workable solutions and to identify the people or institutions that could make those things happen.

Five separate times, our school board was asked to consider sanctioning a task force. At one meeting, it was presented with the differences between the existing committees and their functions, including how a task force would only serve the district for a short time period and in an advisory capacity with no real power. All five times, the school board said "no" while other communities in our state and our own state government moved ahead with similar ideas. The "mechanism for dialogue and action" was to be committees. So, with others that were equally willing to give of themselves, we sat on safe school committee after safe school committee. And, with persistence and patience, some progress was being made. Some issues were being addressed in a comprehensive district plan.

Time ran out on the discrimination lawsuit. Some committees that were part of that lawsuit disbanded. I was invited to join the district Safe and Drug Free Schools committee that met quarterly, early in the morning, with an agenda so packed with presentations that little to no time remained for discussions before heading to work. It no longer met the "collective needs" for me.

On May 1, 2003, a letter was written asking the superintendent what suggestion he might have now on a direction to take to address the original issues of safe and disciplined schools that had been so clearly voiced that fateful April evening in 1999. No answer was provided. This is the point where one must turn to humor to remain sane. Do you know the definition of a committee? The answer: the unwilling, appointing the unknowing, to do the unnecessary. At the time, it was funny.

Four years on these committees and one has to wonder if the results justified the sacrifice of precious time. Improvements had been made at various levels and continue to be made by hard-working, caring individuals. Don't get me wrong. Things are better than they were, in many ways. As a district, we had gone from not wanting to give up an inch of our "site-based" decision making powers, not wanting to even use the word "consistent," to having more consistent policies and common discipline language at all our elementary schools. We agreed that it was necessary because of the high level of mobility within the community. We even use the word "consistency" freely now and in a good way. And we had come up with a plan.

The experts on safe school issues long ago identified the importance of community involvement in planning and the implementation of plans. In this district, the tough issues of respect, fairness, and parental and community roles need readdressing. They were addressed in the original plans. They were good plans. But, honestly, being just a parent, and a working parent at that, one cannot keep pounding away at the administration to stick with the plan. The need for sustained parental oversight most certainly wears a person down. When people's views get ignored, proven ideas get put down, well-constructed plans get forgotten enough times, people give up. I've often wondered if that very idea is some sort of technique or theory they teach in administrative school. It worked on me; a dead end on the issue of safety and discipline had been reached.

Now, the stories come from parents or relatives of children who have been harassed at school to the point that they have to move to a different school or house, have to live with the thought that bullying was a contributing factor to suicide, have had their house shot up in drive-bys, or have a kid who quietly suffers waiting until the day they can get out of the daily "drama" of school. Victims are forced out and the local terrorists, our gangs and bullies, move on to triumph over their next victims.

Reflecting on the current stories (anecdotes) coming out of our schools, it is a statement from 1999 that is haunting. It was from a student attending the meeting on April 20, 1999, who said, "I think it's funny how people can come to meetings and complain, but do you actually see them stepping in and doing something about it?" Our youth know what we need to do. They know that building fences alone won't stop gangs and bullies from doing their damage to society. Will we ever listen to them?

Without a shared vision within our community, our safe schools plans vanished with the changing administration and the changing school board. Our district failed to follow through on its original plans. Other plans now exist but I have yet to see this community have another meaningful open exchange of ideas, on a large scale, about discipline, bullying, and gangs in this "failing" school district.

THE THREE Rs: READING, WRITING, AND ARITHMETIC

Reading is our first and most basic educational process. From kindergarten through third grade, children learn to read. Thereafter they read to learn.

The 90% Reading Goal

If the education system struggles with discipline in the classrooms, some assume that it is just a reflection of the general decline of civility within our society. When classroom disruptions interfere with learning, the blame reflects back on society. With that in mind, the circumstances in our son's first grade class were taken as just such a situation.

Five extremely disruptive boys were added to the mix in this class of twenty-eight students. Halfway through the year, it was decided to break them up by moving two of them out to other rooms. No doubt, continuous disruptions had been a setback for some and outright detrimental to the learning of the Three Rs for others. The fact that something else was to be learned from this experience eluded understanding at the time.

Things were being taught very differently than what my memory served. The general structuring of the class didn't feel right, but, being just a parent unfamiliar with the changes occurring in education, you go with the flow. And being a trusting classroom volunteer, teacher instructions about helping kids were followed unquestionably. Instincts were saying differently but the belief was that teachers know what they are doing.

A blind element of trust existed and no one had clarified what exactly a "pilot program" meant.

This was in 1992. It was obviously a period of experimentation in education in our state and the nation as a whole. This was a classroom being taught using the whole language technique for reading, inventive spelling without corrections for writing, and the touch point math technique for the basis of addition. Some would argue that phonics was being taught along with the whole language.

The obvious phonics instruction in this classroom was the use of headsets with a purchased program and worksheets that went along with that instruction. It looked to be instructional technique that is now commonly called "drill and kill," usually with a note of disdain in the speaker's voice. It insinuates that a fact is "drilled" into a child's mind over and over again until it "kills" the desire to learn. Others associate this type of instruction with rote memorization and the two ideas have been so closely related that they are considered one and the same by many.

The idea behind inventive spelling with no corrections is to minimize any inhibitions to writing. It is to foster creativity and build self-esteem. As volunteers, we were instructed to have the students read their writing to us and praise them. We were to make no corrections; in other words, we were not to instruct them.

Occasionally, uncomfortable moments would arise when kids couldn't remember what they wrote and wondered why you couldn't read what they wrote. They would flash you a look expressing their sentiments ("You dummy!"). That was acceptable and even amusing, but others you could tell felt differently. They were the ones that had written on their faces feelings of disappointment. They didn't do a very good job if an adult reader couldn't read it. Or were they disappointed that we didn't give them more? They are smart.

We should be so smart in choosing how we instruct children. We must consider the potential effect our decisions have on children before we put them into action in the classroom. We should remember that what we do in first grade sets the stage for the reading, writing, and math skills they need for the rest of their lives. Mistakes can be devastating.

Why we thought taking a special education technique like touch point math and applying it to whole classrooms of able students was a good idea is beyond comprehension. It was not a smart decision. Consider your child very lucky if they weren't subjected to this arithmetic "pilot program." This particular group of twenty-eight children got more than their share of pilot programs. In this case, the use of the word "pilot" means that these children served as a "trial unit for experimentation" (*Webster's*, 1976). In any experiment, you run the risk of failure. The big question becomes: How many were set up for future failures because of it?

Going from volunteering one day a week for the first grade class to two days a week the next year helped to foster a new realization. The instincts that brought about an uneasy feeling toward these new instructional techniques may have been correct; things didn't seem right.

But searching for answers wasn't the motivator to volunteer more days; the hope was that this would help free up time for the second grade teacher to provide more much needed individual attention to my own child. It had become obvious that learning differences were emerging.

Well into this second grade year and knowing this group of kids pretty well by then, it was fairly easy to identify who was falling significantly behind in class. Watching these children at work at their desks, some could easily be observed developing coping techniques. They were pretty good at being able to copy someone else's work, even upside-down. That is a skill. At a glance, 20–30 percent of these kids were exhibiting various signs of having learning difficulties. That seemed like a lot of kids. I wanted to know why this was and what would be done. The teacher's response provided insight into what could potentially happen to these kids. She looked at me sadly and said, "I think you are looking at our future dropouts."

Ours was one of them. That is one of those moments when motherly instincts slam smack into the face of reality. The need to concentrate on keeping my own from being part of that statistic became a goal. That class ended up with a state-reported 70 percent graduation rate. But, to put that into perspective, remember that real numbers are difficult to decipher, as are the facts.

Fact: In the Progress in International Reading Literacy Study in 2006, the average score for U.S. fourth grade students was lower than the average of ten other educational systems in the study.

Reading

As a parent, my grasp of the theory behind the whole language concept was that we all become sight readers. You aren't phonetically sounding out every word on this page. You quickly recognize the familiar words and move on. This is something you developed over time probably at your own pace as you became confident with your vocabulary.

The observed trend in the classrooms in the early 1990s was almost the opposite. They were teaching recognition of whole words first and large numbers of words at a time. Paper copies of reading books would be used at school, come home at night, and also be used for testing. They seemed to be expecting the kids to memorize all the words. Looking back, was that "drilling and killing" the interest in reading? How should whole language be taught?

At this time, in the curriculum handbook for our district's teachers, the directive they were given as the number one instruction on strategies to teach when a child didn't recognize a word was "to guess." An instruction to sound out a word was buried near the bottom of the list of reading strategies. And nowhere to be found was encouragement for students to seek to clarify words or explore their meanings if they weren't clear to them.

Sight reading and guessing alone may not sound too bad on the surface; with practice, children should eventually memorize most common words. It is when these groups of kids, taught by this method alone, begin to progress to the next levels that it becomes apparent that no plan is in place as to how or when we make them "guess" correctly if they aren't doing so already. If they aren't given other doable approaches to reading a word, guessing is their only option and it is certainly the quickest and easiest thing to do.

Many children in whole language classrooms do pick up the ability to sound out words accurately. Those lucky kids may be easy learners who really didn't need much instruction to get them reading accurately, or they may have had more instruction at home or with a tutor, or they may have had a teacher who closed the door and ignored the district's directives for instruction and taught phonics. Somehow, some children got the tools they needed to progress.

Some people can't teach phonics. My mother clarified this phenomenon by sharing her observations on phonics in the public school system.

She remembered watching phonics instruction come in and out of the classrooms repeatedly as my six brothers and I had gone through school. She said she could tell which of us had it and which didn't. I believe her.

Of course, that is considered anecdotal. It's just an opinion and from another person that's just a parent without education credentials. Her statement might not mean much to the education elite but it certainly meant a lot to me. It explained my inability to teach our son the phonetic skills he seemed to be missing. How should phonics be taught?

Good fortune presented the opportunity to observe a technique and structure of teaching reading that was totally different than what had been observed in our son's class four years earlier. In our daughter's first grade class, the phonics portion of the instruction process was remarkable. You can't begin to understand it until you hear and watch it being taught by someone that really knows what she is doing.

In this class, the phonics lessons were given with all kids gathered in a small circle at the teacher's feet facing her. This enabled the teacher to observe the shape of the kids' mouths and the position of their tongues as they mimicked the sound that she was making while their eyes were on the letter combinations (blends) that she was teaching.

It's hard to say if the object of these lessons was concentrated on specific blends or more on the idea that kids need to recognize that letters do not always stand alone in a word. This was not an intense effort to drill a particular combination into their heads. It wasn't even followed by a specific book focused on the lesson.

The class would break up into smaller informal groups or on their own to practice what they had learned. We volunteers had been asked to come at this time to be available to read with children that wanted us as part of their group. The teacher was then free to work with individuals that I suspect she was targeting as needing her expertise. We were on hand so the kids could practice with some guidance. If they happened to recognize a letter blend from their lessons, that became exciting for them.

It wasn't apparent from the structure of the instruction that any designation was made of which kids were the top readers and which were the bottom readers. Possibly if you watched the teacher closely enough you would be able to figure it out. That was in total contrast to previous observations where children were almost immediately assigned to leveled reading groups with little hope of ever being in the top group if that wasn't where they started. Kids unfortunately figured that out very quickly. That observation has been noted by multiple parents.

In *Reaching Higher: The Power of Expectations in Schooling*, Rhona S. Weinstein, parent and educator, describes a study of three first grade classrooms. Her findings "revealed remarkably restricted mobility between groups: no member of a low reading group was able to gain entry into the highest reading group" (2002, 53).

Weinstein also made this piercing statement: "That children know whether we think them smart or dull should give us pause" (289). The result of that realization in our son's classroom was at times obvious on the children's faces and reflected in their attitudes. While in our daughter's first grade classroom, when they broke up into groups or individually to read, they decided their own level and the atmosphere of excitement about reading was obvious.

A difference also existed between these two classrooms in the reading material. Our daughter was exposed to stories that were about everyday life and the living things around us. It wasn't Dick, Jane, and Spot, but the themes resembled what you might think of as the modern-day equivalent to those old stories. The kids could relate them to their own lives.

On the other hand, our son had to struggle with nonsensical names and stories about faraway places that he couldn't relate to at all. Those stories may be excellent for established readers but certainly made guessing at words extremely difficult and the goal of reading to learn an iffy prospect.

Writing

The theory that, above all else, we need to protect the self-esteem of students was never more evident than when it came to the teaching of writing during those early 1990s. Don't misunderstand—preserving a child's self-esteem and creativity is important. Children must come out of schools with their natural interest in learning intact. But it only seemed like common sense to make relevant corrections when they are younger rather than forcing them to face what amounts to failure as an adolescent or adult. That was obviously not the consensus in the teaching profession at the time. What is the consensus now?

Listening to children read back what they had written, giving them encouragement, and not making corrections are very reasonable in the beginning. But just like with guessing at a word when reading, at what point do you start to teach accuracy with spelling and grammar? That was a question that should have been asked earlier rather than later, and would have, had not that blinding trust also made us mute.

It would be many years down the road before the realization would become clear that no consistent plan existed in this district for improving the writing skills of all students. A seventh grade English teacher clarified it by saying point blank that no specific plan had been made for these kids that had not acquired the writing skills they should have to that point. She went on to say, "We don't know what to do with them."

In our curriculum, we had lists of frequently used words predetermined by grade that teachers were to teach the kids to spell. This was done in the traditional way of giving the kids a list of words weekly to memorize and then following up with a test on those same words. That is how many an American was taught spelling.

A similar approach was used for grammar lessons in that they were also done out of the context of a written piece. The lessons were done as class work on the board or a worksheet where mistakes would be corrected. Many times it would be an isolated sentence or two written by some unknown about something that may or may not draw the interest of the students.

Writing assignments themselves were infrequent. Over the years, the most commonly observed writing practice was journal writing. Some would argue that a journal is too private an arena in which to do any correcting of spelling or grammar. Let's assume that is correct and then consider: couldn't a journal at least be used to get the students to clarify thoughts, to encourage some questioning by the students themselves, or to demonstrate a deeper thought process, or as a place to encourage them to explore interests?

A quick glance at an old eleventh grade English journal was revealing. The checkmark and good grade indicated that the apparent expectation for eleventh grade English was to be able to write three sentences in a form that looks like a paragraph but not necessarily making a point like a paragraph is supposed to do. No question marks existed where clarification was sorely needed. The absence of comments and marks, other than the checkmark, indicated completion of an entry and no in-depth thought process was necessary to make the grade.

Not correcting anything was only reinforcing mistakes, not teaching good writing habits. Provided with an insufficient number of writing projects, students lacked the opportunities to learn to write adequately and with confidence. This seemed wrong especially when you consider that, when training an animal, repetition with reinforcement of good behavior is the basis for success. If you are forced to make corrections, it is best done when the mistake occurs or as soon as possible thereafter.

The importance of writing and spelling has eluded many. Being just a parent, who wasn't the best with grammar and writing in school and who has always been one of the worst at spelling, it was being part of the workforce that revealed their importance to me. Mathematics and science were my true interests.

Fact: In the 2006 Programme for International Student Assessment, the average score for fifteen-year-old U.S. students was lower than the average of thirty-one other educational systems in mathematics literacy.

Arithmetic

How could we have gone so wrong? So many of us, in so many different ways, went wrong. In your district it may have been "New Math"; in mine it was "Touch Point Math" followed by some "New Math" techniques.

For those of you unfamiliar with touch point math, it is a proven effective method for teaching special education children who have been judged to be incapable of learning to add any other way. It is where the correct number of dots and circles are located on the number itself. For example, the number 8 has four dots which are surrounded by four circles. The child learns to touch and count the dots and circles and uses that method to add numbers.

What appears to have happened when this was used in non–special education classrooms was that a noticeable number of these children clung to this method as a crutch and, in the end, it slowed them down. Teachers began to notice the difference in test scores. If you watched a child in the classroom you could tell when they were counting incrementally to get an answer for simple addition. As the numbers that they were adding got bigger, the technique made the process of getting an answer painfully slow.

In all fairness to the technique, what may have also contributed to our district's failing math scores were the curriculum instructions to decrease attention to the rote memorization of math facts. So, if you hadn't learned what nine plus nine equals, you could start at nine and count nine dots and circles. What would you do if you had no confidence in your ability to recall an answer?

For whatever reason, the detrimental effects of failed math instruction techniques became obvious through classroom observations as the same group of kids advanced through the grade levels. It didn't matter what test we were using to track them; the scores were falling and later failing to make the grade.

In the upper grades, teachers didn't seem to know how to go about reversing this downward trend while some teachers in the lower grades acted as if it really wasn't a big deal. If those teachers weren't communicating with any upper-level math teachers then they weren't hearing what the upper-level teachers had to say about the poor performance of the students they were receiving. The elementary teacher would only know that the children seemed to be able to add and subtract at a first, second, or third grade level.

When our district finally dropped the touch point pilot program, the need for our school board to address the issue was long overdue. They deserved to be applauded for dropping that particular pilot program, but they needed to address plans to correct the problems that this technique had created for certain students. What do you do when an experiment goes wrong?

Scattered throughout this community were parents who were thinking that their child wasn't good at math. The parents had no way of knowing that their child may potentially have succumbed to a mistake in the teaching technique. After approaching our school board to answer the question of what to do next, their response came in a "thank you for your time and concern" letter. No action was taken to try to correct the problem the schools had created with this pilot program.

These unfortunate kids may forever have numbers in their brains that have dots and circles on them and they may continue to use them. If they had been cars, a recall would have been forthcoming. In medicine, if you make a mistake, you attempt to correct it as soon as possible because you know it will snowball on itself. They don't do that in education; they just pass on their failures. And we moved on.

In mathematics instruction, we moved on to the next fad. This one seems to have been more widespread in the United States. The theory is to introduce multiple concepts and come back to revisit and reteach them on a regular basis. At this point, the trust was gone and skepticism was the new order of the day. Every aspect of every change deserved to be looked at with a critical eye.

The work papers and tests with this new program did not physically have enough room on them for anyone with crude fine motor skills to show their work. Teachers allowed students to just put an answer without showing their work, thus making it difficult for upper-level algebra teachers to later break that bad habit. Nowhere did it appear that we were teaching kids to check their work, every time. And where this teaching technique really appeared to fail kids was in the fact that they didn't seem to do enough of any one type of problem to master it and cement it concretely in their minds.

This time, the intuition of this parent was confirmed in a scientific study known as the Third International Math and Science Study or TIMSS report. Since that time, the word "Third" has been replaced with the words "Trends in" to still keep the initials TIMSS. One conclusion of its chief investigators was that when we, in the United States, think about the basics we think of repeating concepts over and over. In other countries outperforming us in math and science, they consider that "the basics are so important that when they are introduced, the curriculum focuses on them. They are given concentrated attention so that they can be mastered, and children can be prepared to learn a new set of different basics in following grades" (Valverde & Schmidt, 1997–1998, 63). That definitely fits the correlations made based on observations about math, but what about science?

CHAPTER THREE
WHERE'S THE SCIENCE?

Students should develop a conceptual understanding of the natural world, critical-thinking skills, and scientific habits of mind, including curiosity, respect for evidence, flexibility of perspective, and an appreciation for living things.

South Carolina LASER Institute (2002)

Consider yourself among the fortunate if your children experienced an adequate amount of hands-on science teaching in their elementary school. And your children are extremely fortunate if that practice continued throughout their middle school and high school careers. This is not the case consistently across the United States. That fact became painfully clear through experiences within my local education system.

After several years of volunteering in classrooms, it started to become apparent that little to no science was being taught in many of the elementary classes. Conversations about the topic would include such remarks from teachers as: "We don't have time in the day" or "We don't have the equipment to do it." From the parents you would hear, "The teachers don't like to teach science" or "They don't feel comfortable teaching science."

A trip to the district office was in order. The question to the then–acting superintendent was "Do we have a science curriculum?" His answer: "Our kids are good in science." Was that really the case?

At this point in time, our district was using the Iowa Test of Basic Skills (ITBS) and the first time it was given to children was in the their third grade year. On our son's first test, the area he scored highest in was science. It appeared the acting superintendent was right. In some unknown way, our school must have been doing a good job teaching science.

Years went by, and the now yearly ITBS scores were recorded, put in the student's file, and a copy sent home to the parents. As a parent, on a standardized national test like these, you at least wanted to see your child hold his ranking. Our son's percentile ranking in the United States had actually been steadily rising in language and reading, dramatically rising in math (after some unteaching and reteaching), but steadily dropping in science. The ITBS was last given in his seventh grade year where his score in science was twenty percentile points below where he had started in the ranking in third grade.

How much emphasis a person should put on test results is questionable but this looked like a red flag waving. It was time to carefully watch what was going on in the science classes. For the next three years, as a junior high and high school parent who was no longer wanted as a volunteer, watching became difficult and could not possibly reveal the whole picture. The problems that were prominent were both unbelievable and unforgivable. It's doubtful that any single situation was unique to this school and this moment in time but the hope would be that such a combination of things happening to one kid was just bad luck. Keep in mind, every situation our son encountered was what approximately 150 of his classmates also experienced.

Eighth grade brought an experience with a first-time teacher attempting to teach physical science without even a model of an atom in the room. She honestly was trying to do the best she could with very little in the way of materials to do her job. She basically ended up using the "drill-and-kill" instructional method. She sent home the science vocabulary words, had the children memorize them even if the words made no sense, and then expected them to regurgitate them on a test. At home, the best that could be done was to try to lend some understanding and relevancy to the words. Perhaps a complaint should have been made to the principal or higher-ups, but experience thus far had taught that you more than likely would not see the problem resolved in a timely fashion. And besides, this situation wasn't this teacher's fault and potentially she could have been blamed. She didn't return to our district the next year.

That next year brought a new subject, with an experienced teacher, but the same "drill-and-kill" technique. To add relevancy to earth science is tricky when a person has no expertise in the subject or any previous interest in it. To be accurate and helpful, a book at home was necessary. When the teacher was asked about a book coming home, the answer was "There aren't enough books for kids to take them home." The arrangement was that kids were to come to the classroom after school, check out a book, and make sure it was back before school the next morning. But the teacher was also a coach and wasn't always available after school to check the books out. After jostling with that situation in the fall, a book was finally assigned to us.

When it was time to study for the cumulative final in this class, it seemed to be the perfect opportunity to demonstrate how a person can make use of previous tests to pinpoint areas of study where they should focus their attention. Since the answer sheets but never the tests themselves came home with the student, we went in after school one day and asked the teacher if we could go over the previous tests. He said he had already gotten rid of them; he was moving to a new room the next year. Frustration and disappointment had a battle to see who reigned supreme. The moment to teach a useful study skill, a teaching moment, was shattered. But that year still didn't compare in frustration level to the next.

His biology class was being taught by a coach in his last year of teaching. No syllabus was used to inform us or the student about the subjects to be covered and when. Few class notes existed and, again, no book that could come home. The tests were all essay without a guide as to what they were graded on and, again, they never came home. Our son was getting a good grade. But of more importance was the answer to the question "Was he getting a good biology education?" Although in later years temptation would rise up, this was the one and only time we ever pulled either of our kids from a class. All that could be said was "Enough!"

What may have added to the unbearable intolerance of this situation was a revelation during the previous summer. An administrator had given my name to a high school science teacher working on a grant to attend a K–8 Science Education Strategic Planning Institute in South Carolina. Along with a team of teachers and the superintendent, the job of the designated community scientist was to bring back information to the community and stimulate interest in science education. In June of 2002, this institute made clear to us the ideals behind quality science instruction.

The title of the institute was Leadership and Assistance for Science Education Reform (LASER) and was based on the National Science Resources Center (NSRC) model of systemic science education reform. The teaching philosophy behind what this institute was promoting was that children learn science best in an inquiry-centered environment. For those of us without education credentials, this translates to giving a child something to work on or with and allowing their natural curiosity and interest to guide them in asking and answering questions. In other words, we parents might call it "hands-on" learning.

Using a variety of lectures and activities, the institute presented the important concepts behind understanding and establishing quality science instruction. Topics stretched from brain development to the essential factors in changing a local education system. Its goal was to teach us how we can help students become problem solvers using critical thinking skills while learning relevant science facts. The goal of the institute was to have districts come away with a plan to improve the teaching of science in their district.

We met the goal of the institute. We did come away with a plan and we thought it was a good plan. Unfortunately for the kids in our district, economics and politics would prevent this team from implementing the plan. Our daughter, even though she trailed her brother by years, would not see any benefit from the knowledge gained or the efforts of this team to improve science education instruction in our district. However, years later an opportunity to use a small portion of what had been learned at that institute would present itself.

In the fall of 2006, inquiry led to information about a federal grant administered through our state's Department of Education. It was a Math and Science Partnership Program grant aimed at professional development, which is another term for teacher training. At the time, this appeared to be an opportunity to practice partnership building skills and use the previously gained knowledge of science education at the same time.

The situation in our district at this time was that the administration was severely limiting the amount of time teachers could spend on anything other than reading, language arts, and math due to our poor performance on our state's tests. We hadn't started testing for science yet. Our school district is surrounded by districts that were teaching science starting in the elementary grades using the best practices of hands-on techniques. These surrounding districts were performing better on the standardized tests in reading and math.

Curiosity and an inquiring nature leads one to ask: Were they performing better and as a result had the luxury of teaching science, or were they performing better because they had been teaching science in a way that stimulated the naturally curious young brain, making learning in reading and math more relevant, interesting, and therefore more productive? In the end, the hope was that the readers of our grant would be thinking along the same lines.

To even begin this grant process, a partnership needed to be developed between an institute of higher learning and a school or school district labeled as "failed" by No Child Left Behind rules. Then, according to what had been learned about the change process at the LASER institute and based on the NSRC theory of action, we needed to establish a common knowledge of research and best practices among the key leaders in this project. Together, we needed to develop a common vision for moving forward with science education at the elementary level in the district.

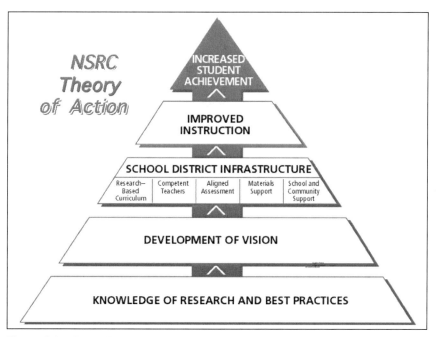

Figure 3.1. Reproduction here is with the permission of the National Science Resource Center. This diagram cannot be reproduced in any form without the expressed written permission of the NSRC.

Three months later, we had completed the grant writing project and had built an excellent team that would be ready to work should we be awarded the grant. The main writers consisted of the knowledgeable principal of our "failed" downtown school, a very brave education professor from our local private college, and myself. As part of the larger team, we had several elementary teachers, both middle schools represented by science teachers, and a district administrator that was becoming very open to the idea. That, in itself, was a huge accomplishment.

We began this endeavor knowing it was a competitive process. In our state, they would be awarding three to four grants. The grant proposals were being sent to evaluators outside the state to ensure fairness in judging them with the final decision being made at the state level. We were reassured, as postelection State Department of Education personnel changed, that the evaluators had been hired ahead of the changeover of administration and all was a "go" for the process to proceed as previously indicated and in a timely fashion.

Our grant proposal, *Bringing Science into the Elementary Classroom*, was ranked second overall in the state by the independent evaluators. In defense of that ranking not being first place, we would have scored higher had the out-of-state evaluators connected with the fact that we had no baseline state statistics in science because we had yet to develop those tests. We were not awarded the grant. The number of awards to be given had supposedly been cut.

The reality for us was that new personnel in the State Department of Education had worked with a math partnership in our district previously and math trumped science, no matter how good the proposal. As with many situations that are tied to politics, somebody knew somebody. Our partnership got the proverbial political shaft. But one does need to face the facts.

The grant proposal had failed to demonstrate to our state administration the importance of inquiry science education and its direct correlation to the improvement of math and reading scores. So, in no way did they even come close to comprehending the importance of inquiry science education in the development of young minds and their future ability to think critically and apply their education in the sciences for the betterment of our social and economic needs.

Medicine, energy usage, and climate change are all perfect examples of the relationship between social and economic needs and quality science education. Talk abounds about improving the health care system in the United States but not nearly enough of it is about real preventive health care. In veterinary medicine, especially in the food production fields, the debate no longer exists that responsible preventive medicine costs less than treatment of illnesses and the loss in productivity that sick animals experience.

The key to effective preventive medicine is education. When you apply that idea of educating people to the economics of wise use of resources, consider how much better off we would have been when gas prices were over four dollars per gallon if people had previously been better educated about energy consumption.

We must consider education's potential as a powerful tool in helping to alter the direction of climate change. If all people understood and applied just the basics of conservation of natural resources, the situation would dramatically improve. Clearly, we must address science education issues to address the social issues of health care, energy usage, and our world environment.

The humor of the situation can be found in irony. The tunnel vision produced by standards and testing for reading and math had limited or excluded the use of quality classroom science education as a potential tributary to success. We were forced to teach to the test. In the 20/20 hindsight we all have, seeing "No Child Left Behind" on the title page of that grant application, we should have known better than to have gotten involved.

Fact: In the 2006 Programme for International Student Assessment, the average score for fifteen-year-old U.S. students was lower than the average of twenty-two other educational systems in scientific literacy.

CHAPTER FOUR
ALONG CAME "NO CHILD LEFT BEHIND"

A school cannot be studied satisfactorily, nor judged fairly, except in terms of its own philosophy of education, its individually expressed purposes and objectives, the nature of the pupils with which it has to deal, and the needs of the community which it serves.

Cooperative Study of Secondary School Standards

Standards and Testing

B efore the No Child Left Behind law came into existence, our state and our local school district were attempting to straighten out the mess that had been created during the most recent downturn in various test scores. They were coming to the conclusion that statistics truly were showing that problems now existed as a result of allowing the teaching pendulum to swing too far in favor of experimenting with teaching techniques that had gone wrong.

The state and local education agencies were starting to make what looked to be real improvements as they were coming to an understanding of where they went wrong and attempting to adjust accordingly. The process was proceeding at a snail's pace but it was slowly floating forward. Then along came exit standards testing. Suddenly, we were going to hold the student accountable by denying them a high school diploma if they failed the exit standards test.

The theory behind it really does sound reasonable when you think about it. The idea is that we develop a set of standards that we can basically agree on as to what we would like all graduates to know and be able to do before receiving a diploma. This was supposed to ensure that a high school diploma really meant something more than the fact that students attended school—what some refer to as "seat time." It was to ensure that a basic set of skills were developed in each student, and the high school diploma would serve as a testament to that fact.

In my state the skills had been defined, many years before this, in Idaho Code 33-1612 mentioned previously as defining a *Thorough System of Public Schools*. Those skills were identified and stated as "the skills necessary to communicate effectively; the skills necessary for students to enter the work force; the skills to enable them to be responsible citizens of their homes, schools and communities." In addition, this law states that "schools will provide a basic curriculum necessary to enable students to enter academic or professional-technical postsecondary educational programs" and that they will be "introduced to current technology."

The writers of this law did an excellent job of defining what the people (the business community, parents, and community in general) want from their public school system. The question becomes whether or not anyone at the State Board or Departments of Education or our local school board read and understood these words. They obviously didn't keep its ideals in the forefront when planning their next move.

Considering the fact that my state was many years behind other states in this "exit standards" process, it would have been easy to learn from other states about both their mistakes and their successes. We proceeded by first writing our own set of standards for language arts, math, science, health, and social studies. This was done through committees of chosen people, along with taking comments at some not-so-well publicized public meetings.

The developed standards were taken to the state legislature in 2000 for its approval, and the first class to be held accountable to pass this new testing was slated to be the class of 2005, our first child's graduating class. Being one of the few parents knowing intimately what that class's learning experiences had consisted of sealed the obligation to testify at the State Joint Legislative Education Committee Hearings.

Careful preparation was called for given the fact that they may only allow about three minutes for a person to voice their view. Thoughts on the experiences of the past nine years needed to be condensed. The message needed to open their eyes to the existence of poor learning environments, poor teaching techniques, or lack of instruction in some subject areas, and the lack of proven effective remedies for problems that the aforementioned had created. The intention was to try to put the legislators in the shoes of a "failing" child of the class of 2005.

At this point, in 2000, these students had been in the school system for eight years. In the next five years, according to the State Board's proposal, we would be able to identify the problems of each individual and address those problems with "research proven effective remediation." Remediation means "to find a remedy." We were only at the point where we could admit in our own minds that mistakes had been made. We had yet to say out loud that some experiments went wrong. How do you find a remedy when you won't discuss all the causes?

We were actually being asked to put our faith in the system's ability to identify and fix problems it had partially created itself. Numerous teachers in the upper grades had no idea why their students were coming to them unprepared. It was like a dirty little well-kept secret. Certainly, parents and the public weren't informed. As a parent, I never got a "recall for faulty instruction" notice. How could a student be held accountable by denying them a diploma when nobody had openly admitted that mistakes had been made, let alone worked cooperatively to correct them?

Just before the testimony started, the chairman announced that they would not take comments on implementation of the standards, only on the standards themselves. Putting aside the much-rehearsed outline that mainly addressed implementation, finding a copy of the standards, and going through it like a mad woman with a marker, a new approach to deliver the message was devised. Improvise.

First, the message was politely delivered that some of us had come prepared to talk about implementation of the standards and the testing and would be looking forward to addressing that subject at a different time in the future. A nod came from the chairman indicating that input on implementation would occur at another time but it was apparently not a promise. That opportunity never came; implementation of standards never received its public hearing with the legislature.

After all testimony had been given that morning, the room emptied into the hallway where the chairperson's secretary seemed to go out of her way to deliver the following observation: "If they were listening, they got your message." For what had been expressed to the legislature was a comparison: a compliment on each specific, well-intentioned, relevant standard followed by a statistic or observation to point out where the average students really were at this point in time in relation to that particular standard. The hope was that a light would go on and it would dawn on them how unrealistic it would be to get these students to the desired level in such a short time. The object was not to say that standards aren't a good thing. The point was that if exit standards testing was the direction that they were bent on going, the students needed the standards and curriculum in place eight years ago!

The legislature was apparently not listening to the few of us that were in attendance without a political or monetary agenda. Our state then proceeded to hire a testing company that was inexperienced in exit standards testing. The testing company, along with the State Board, held some, again, not-so-well-publicized public meetings. The principal of the middle school where our local class of 2005 was attending was asked if a notification could be distributed through his school to the parents informing them of this meeting. His response was "It is not my responsibility to inform parents about educational issues."

So it goes. The testing floodgates were opened with a resultant current too strong to swim against alone. No good way to reach others who might have cared to help could be found. I attended that meeting as the lone self-appointed representative of our students. An employee of the testing company came up afterward to tell me to "fight the good fight," for even many of them did not believe in "exit testing." With disappointment imminent, without very large numbers of parents knowing and understanding what was happening, it was too hard to prevail; it was impossible to fight. The people promoting this project were so sure of themselves; they didn't need to listen to the voices of the scores of dissenters from all over the area and across the education spectrum that had voiced similar concerns.

Keep in mind that in 2000 this was referred to as "high stakes testing." A diploma was what was at stake. If you don't consider that a high stake, look at the difference in the earning potential of those with and without a high school diploma. And remember, at the time it was also referred to as exit standards testing. In many states, this process associated with exit testing had caused a public backlash.

Before No Child Left Behind (NCLB) came fully on the scene, the spinmeisters worked their magic on the name of the testing. It became "standards achievement testing." Everybody wants achievement to occur. Everyone wants standards set to achieve. Nobody can argue that, can they? That would be like going against motherhood and apple pie. Significant resistance had been averted with a change in wording. What we don't know or understand can't hurt us.

We treaded water and waited to see what decisions would be made for us next; anxiety about the future was welling up while we wondered if they would really deny diplomas—if they would really allow the torrent that had been unleashed to wipe out the undeserving students. The wait wasn't long. It was truly amazing to see how quickly the system could change when the right people said "go."

By the summer of 2001, our Assessment and Accountability Commission proposed the rules for our standards achievement test. Their recommendations clearly stated that students who failed the test could still be eligible to graduate if local districts decide to issue them diplomas based on alternate routes to graduation. That left the debate about the true worth of a high school diploma up to the local district. In a school district labeled as "failed," can you deny anyone a diploma that has put in their time without risk of a lawsuit? That is a debate that never openly took place in my district.

So, in the end, the objective of the development of standards achievement testing went from giving value to a diploma to identifying the child's needs and addressing it in their instruction, right? That sounds good. That sounds like what should go on in every classroom every day. But, now being a skeptic, doubts were overflowing. How this was going to work would all be in how it was implemented, and that hadn't been openly discussed.

At that point in 2001, as a taxpayer, the big question at the local school board budget hearings was: "How much money would be set aside for remedial instruction for those failing to pass our new state tests?" At that time, blank stares and shrugs exchanged between the school board members and the superintendent answered the question. There was no money set aside. The money for the purpose of addressing individual students' needs as identified on the new tests wouldn't be designated until this district's 2007 budget.

As a parent, I went from closely following my oldest child's standardized test scores through the fall of 2001 to being totally in the dark while they piloted the new tests. I watched him and his classmates once more become guinea pigs for the system. I anguished as they spent precious instructional time testing those students two and three times a year.

In the fall of 2003, the targeted class of 2005 emerged from the darkness with their ACT scores. It indicated, as did the state tests, that our son could use some additional help. However, the district could not provide any instruction specific to our son's needs. He wasn't bad enough compared to the others in his class. Sound like a child left behind?

At that time, since they had no intention of doing anything beneficial with his test results, a request was made that they not waste his time any further with testing. But, due to poor communications within the school, he was tested again, prompting an angry letter to our State Board of Education. That letter stated: "You were responsible for setting in motion the testing of the children in the class of 2005. You took away a portion of their instructional time and gave them nothing in return. Once again, the education system used children for experimentation without benefit to them. These children have been cheated. You're just lucky most parents don't know enough to realize it." To the then-governor of our state went a letter saying, "Please tell me where the accountability for the administration fits into achievement testing." That request still hangs in the air.

Apparently, the public education resources to help a child being left behind were in reality nonexistent or had been exhausted (like myself). Where does one turn for help within the public education system?

How "No Child Left Behind" Works (or Doesn't)

In the fall of 2004, the machinery behind No Child Left Behind was in full gear. If you were a parent with a child in a school that had been labeled as "needs improvement," you received a letter required as part of the NCLB sanctions. This was part of the penalty for not scoring well on the new standardized tests. Our letter read: "Under federal and state laws and rules, students in schools identified for improvement are eligible to apply for transfer to another school within the district that has met state academic goals. However, our district has no transfer options available at this time because we have only one high school in our district." In this case, instead of a sanction meaning a penalty, it obviously meant "the act of a recognized authority confirming an action" (*Webster's*, 1976). It confirmed our need for help and it only took three years to do it.

An interpretation of this letter is that you are stuck in a failed school unless you have the money to move or attend private school, or the time, energy, and commitment to start a charter school or have one available and get selected, or you desire to home school. Within this public school system, this letter just affirmed that we were sending our child to a "failed" school; it changed nothing. In the future, similar letters would be delivered again and again.

So, let's see if we can review this briefly and make sense of what happened. Each state, independently, for the most part, spent time and money developing standards, developing tests, and in some cases redeveloping tests, used students' instructional time to validate the tests, and used the results to put in place (in this case) meaningless sanctions such as letters to parents from schools that "failed" repeatedly. Now, what exactly is No Child Left Behind?

From the perspective of a parent who has suffered through trying to answer this question without actually reading the law, it can be said with certainty that it is a federal law over nine hundred pages long that was passed in 2001. One should at this point question whether most lawmakers read and/or understood it. The reason we should wonder is not its length alone, but also the fact that it sets as its goal that all students, 100 percent, will be proficient in all tested subject areas by 2014.

The thought behind that is certainly an appealing one. Who wouldn't like to see us shooting for 100 percent proficient students? Proficient means "highly competent, skilled or adept" (*Webster's*, 1976). That definitely sounds like what people want in our students, 100 percent; no doubt. We can give 100 percent of our students an effective education relevant to their needs. However, consider whether, when dealing with people in the arena of statistics, we frequently get 100 percent on anything? What were our representatives thinking? And we chose to measure this competency or skill based on what and how?

Well, we go back to those standards that were set for us and those achievement tests that in our state started out as grand plans to assess skills and ended up being the same old multiple choice–type test done on a computer to collect a score. How does this differ from the old standardized tests of the past? With the current standards tests we were supposed to use the results to tailor the instruction to the students' needs. We saw how that worked in 2004. What we need to further understand is not what the scores mean, but what this law was intended to do.

We must look back to President Lyndon Johnson's "War on Poverty." The Elementary and Secondary Education Act (ESEA) of 1965 was passed as part of that war because of the sentiment that the needs of children living in poverty were not being met by state and local officials. The ESEA is reviewed by Congress at least every five to six years. No Child Left Behind is the 2001 reauthorization plan for this 1965 law.

But back to the current NCLB law itself. Based on what a school's original proficiency level was when first tested and finding the difference from 100 percent (its goal), a school's yearly goal is then calculated by dividing that difference by the number of years to the target year 2014. That is one way an annual yearly progress (AYP) goal can be determined, but it may be set differently depending on where you live. Your state may also decide that it won't increase the goal yearly.

Your school's test results are further broken down into twelve subgroups of student demographics to ensure that no particular group of children gets left behind, thus clarifying the name No Child Left Behind. A school needs to make progress toward its yearly goal in all categories. When schools don't meet those goals, they have "failed" to pass their AYP and are labeled as "needs improvement."

As NCLB proceeds, the public is beginning to hear and will hear more about how all schools will become "failed" schools; more and more schools are being labeled as "needs improvement," insinuating failure. The public will hear that being labeled as "failed" doesn't mean what it implies. That is true. That is what happens in cases like this when you set 100 percent as a goal.

Eventually, almost all schools miss the mark. You will hear that you can easily get the "failed" label by missing the goal in one subgroup or by a few students. That is true. But what about a school that failed large numbers of students from the beginning in multiple categories and is given chance after chance after chance? That is a school truly in trouble. And when it is a high school where a diploma is given by an alternate route after failing the standards tests, that school graduates students that are children left behind.

The NCLB law allows schools to fail to pass their AYP for two years in a row before being labeled "needs improvement." NCLB began to count the test scores in 2002. Our district's only high school failed to meet its goals in

2002 and 2003, so we got our first NCLB parent letters in the fall of 2004. That same year, ninth graders were brought into what was originally built to be a three-year high school. When you fail to succeed with some students, making a school bigger by adding more to the mix is allowable?

The logic is baffling, but under NCLB law it was considered a re-configuration and gave the school an additional year to fail and not face additional consequences. So, in 2007, we received the notification required of schools that have failed for three years in a row, when in actuality it had been five years in a row.

This newest letter stated that "The district must make available additional help for eligible students upon parent request." This help is referred to as supplemental services. Three months into the 2007 school year, the district hadn't had a single request for services, yet. The letter went on to indicate that the services would be allotted based on income level and how far the allotted money would spread. It didn't say that no child would be left behind.

With each letter came more unanswered questions. Honestly, it doesn't seem right to bother school board representatives with numerous questions about the law when they are acting as unpaid volunteers, such as they are in my district. Logically, a call to the paid state educational agency employees would be in order.

First, they were asked to confirm that the statistics were correct in that our high school had never passed its annual yearly progress goals. Finding the person that should know was not easy. The fact that it took a lot of time with each person in the chain of command to verify the truth revealed that not enough people were paying attention to the reality of who had failed from the beginning and repeatedly.

So, what about accountability? NCLB is a federal law implemented by the states. Who is supposed to be watching at the state level? The first year of "needs improvement" status requires that a two-year improvement plan be developed. In the past, our school plans were approved after being presented to our school board. Having attended most regular school board meetings for many years, it was evident that our high school had not written its own plan using the process and manner in which the law had intended. Our state department of education wasn't really sure who was responsible for reading those plans and they referred the inquiry to the State Board of Education, which tried to refer it back to the state department. Since no one could be found that had actually read the improvement plan at that time, it was time to get a copy.

After reading it, it was apparent that nobody had read it very well, if at all, since goals had failed to even be set. They really had forgotten or omitted goals in most subject areas; blanks were obvious where goals should have been found. Really! When asked again who was accountable, state officials either explained that it was up to the local school board or they quit returning phone calls. After all, when you are just a parent, you don't carry much weight, even though they tell you "you are important." So, with nowhere to go but up, the U.S. Department of Education was next on the list.

On the first call to them in the fall of 2007, upon inquiring about the complaint process, the response was that no complaint process for No Child Left Behind existed. The second time, upon request, the comments were supposedly noted and passed on to the Secretary of Education. The helpful person answering the phone did confirm the fact that my local school board is ultimately responsible. The conversation also established that, indeed, my state was supposed to identify its failing schools.

So, when you put together all these conversations, it really becomes clear that we have armies of well-paid bureaucrats set up to administer the No Child Left Behind law but, when it comes down to accountability for implementation of the plan, it's a local control issue. It is the implementation of a huge plan that we at the local level were never given a chance to critique. The effectiveness of NCLB depends on, in our case, unpaid local school board members. What else should we know?

Under NCLB law, if your school fails a fourth year in a row, in addition to the sometimes nonexistent school choice and the supplemental services for those comprehending and acting on their right to make that request, the school may be required to replace "certain staff" or "fully implement a new curriculum." If your school moves on to a fifth year in a row, which technically in our district we had long ago surpassed, it is supposedly required to "restructure." What restructuring may mean is that the school may be closed and may be reopened as a charter school; it may be required to replace all or most of the school staff or turn over school operations either to the state or to a private company with a "demonstrated record of effectiveness." You may be thinking that, after all the bungling that has occurred in some schools, it is about time someone else took charge. Think again and real hard about how scary that last step really sounds.

Whether or not you are a big believer in conspiracy theories, you have to think twice. Years ago in a conversation with one of my brothers, the talk drifted to something along the lines of "either these people in power toying with education are really stupid or just evil and greedy." We decided it was probably a combination of both.

With that dialogue echoing in my mind and someone else's words about the "dismantling of the public education system" resonating loudly as I read about the fifth year's sanctions, I have to wonder where we are headed next with No Child Left Behind and our public education system in general.

CHAPTER FIVE
WHAT IS THE PROBLEM?

When we leave the natural method, and adopt a fixed program, and insist upon uniform required subjects, and draw in large numbers of students, then we are tempted to introduce rules, organization, discipline and bribes. Then, education becomes a ritual, not an adventure.

Ralph Waldo Emerson

A whole system has developed around educating children. We call it a system, anyway, and most will continue to do so out of habit. A better descriptor would be a bureaucracy, which *Webster's* defines as "the administration of government through departments and subdivisions managed by sets of appointed officials following an inflexible routine." A system would imply that it is working in "a unified way in an orderly form so as to show a logical plan linking the various parts" (*Webster's*, 1976). The word "system" better describes our ideals in public education rather than the current reality for many of us.

This educational bureaucracy we have created includes the president of the United States, both houses of Congress, the Supreme Court and lower courts, the secretary of education, the U.S. Department of Education, each state's department of education and board of education, the school district administration, and ultimately the local school district board. Along the way, some everyday people may occasionally be a piece of the decision making process. The total cost to keep our education system flowing, from top to bottom, is one fact that we should know but are probably better off not facing, right now. It's sufficient to understand that the distribution of educational opportunity in this country is through an educational bureaucracy that is huge and complicated and supposed to be largely based on state control and the idea of local control.

Local control is a grand idea. The theory is that the people at the local level know what they need and are best able to exert control, direction, and change at that level. They, the people, become the built-in accountability factor. That accountability factor, we the people, is a virtue in the concept of localism.

The flaw in the local control concept is that it is based on the vigilance of we the people. It requires that people be watchful, informed, involved, and vocal. Therein lies the problem, in various ways.

Local control can go wrong. Community members can organize around their own agenda and be successful. Take sports, for example. A group of well-meaning parents can push for administration and board members to be selected based on favorable attitudes toward sports. If those selected to carry out the sports agenda do not have satisfactory attitudes toward and knowledge about academics, academics suffer. For that very reason, some education experts don't trust communities with being able to establish effective schools on their own. Without constant vigilance by the community, you can see the justification in their thinking.

Vigilance means more than just looking out for your own child. It takes looking out for the children of your neighbors, friends, and relatives. It takes people that care about the next generation—that is, really care, not just give the idea of caring lip service, using it as a sound bite, or tossing around the now-standard rhetoric like "no child left behind."

The public education system is great where the local control concept is functioning well. When all the factors necessary for the local control system to function in education's favor are in place, it works. If even some of the ingredients of success are present, there is hope. But, when all factors falter, we find "failed" schools. We find kids going under, going down with no life preserver in sight. When local control of education fails, children have been, do, and will continue to get left behind.

Early in my battle over safe and disciplined school issues, I came to believe that three major factors led to the declining state of our local schools. Those factors are: (1) lack of accountability of administration,

(2) no "checks and balances" provided by the school board, and (3) apathy and the "me and mine" attitude of the public.

Accountability of Administration

Accountability means you are "obligated to be responsible for or able to explain your actions" (*Webster's*, 1976). Administrators are people whose job it is to manage or direct the affairs of an institution. Laws governing the schools, and now standards, are set by the government. And policies and curriculum are approved by the local school boards. School administrators manage the people carrying out the rules. They are managers. They should be accountable to all those above and below them in the hierarchy of the school system. Their actions must be based on the rules they are responsible for carrying out. They shouldn't make their own rules.

Observations, during the dealings with the safe and disciplined schools issues in 1999, lead to the conclusion that many times the administrators didn't know or understand policies or laws. It is their job to know the rules under which they must function. In questioning the administration for clarification of the rules, you run the risk of setting up barriers between yourself and them. Ever feel like walls are going up between you and the person from whom you expect answers?

If administrators do not feel obligated to give explanations to those below them, like we parents are seen to be, you are forced to give up or go around or go above them for your answers. If you choose to persist in seeking the facts, you may encounter the walls building ever higher and the wagons may circle. You may be made to feel like the enemy for asking questions.

Human nature explains this behavior to some extent, in that many times a person views comments as criticism and may take it personally as a direct reflection on them. The scope of this phenomenon and its potential detrimental effects to the education system were not apparent until after reading *Parental Involvement and the Political Principle* by Seymour Sarason.

Dr. Sarason explains that the political principle justifying parental involvement is the belief that, when decisions are made affecting you or your possessions, you should have a role, a voice in the process of that decision making. He describes the "rigid boundaries professionals erect to insure that 'outsiders' remain outsiders." He refers to this behavior as the "cult of professionalism" and uses the example of medical doctors to clarify this point. In that example, he tries to get you to view the political principle when you were "the 'outsider' trying to get an 'insider professional' to take your ideas, feelings, and recommended actions seriously" (1995, 26).

Accountability won't happen when the person asking for it is seen as someone whose experiences or desires are not relevant to the decision-making process. When explanations aren't to be found and no one hears your views or listens to your argument to support your views, you have hit a brick wall. Breaking down that barrier created by the cult of professionalism is too tall an order for just one parent. In the hierarchy of school systems, your local school board should be able to help.

The "Checks and Balances" of the School Board

If you recall, our local school board was asked five separate times to be part of spearheading a community group to explore safety and discipline issues and solutions. They said "no" for reasons that to this day are not fully clear. They threw up a barrier to letting others be a part of the decision-making process. The cult of professionalism includes more people than what fits the technical definition of professionals. The cult appears to have been in play at this level, with this school board, also. However, this particular school board was actually very effective in many ways compared to what followed.

Most recent members of our school board have not been sticking with the job for more than two terms and several did not even finish one term. This turnover seriously affected the functioning of our board, given the large amount of information they should absorb and understand. The learning curve is steep, especially in the beginning and with the changes in our laws. Thinking back over the reasons for the comings and goings of our local school board members could make for a book in itself. We had a member unseated by a challenger whose child, along with friends, got caught drinking beer at an away game. That same new member saw through the demise of the administrator that enforced the admittedly wrongful alcohol policy. Another member sought a seat on the board to get rid of a softball coach while yet another used his power to promote sports in general and a friend, in particular, to high places.

It appeared that the board members understood their power, all right. That position gives them the authority to control others. We would hope, we trust, that they would use that power to make decisions based on knowledge gained and analysis of the issues at hand for the betterment of education for all. For them to make excellent decisions, it would seem logical to seek more than one source of information or perhaps even listen to more than one point of view. They, like many elected people in positions of power, may not have heard the Thomas Jefferson quotation, "Difference of opinion leads to enquiry, and enquiry to truth."

To follow Jefferson's line of reasoning would require that the board members actually take the time to listen to differing views, possibly even seek out different opinions and ask questions to seek to find the truth. To find direction as a board, discussion would be necessary, as a board. If the board bases its decisions only on the information provided to it by administration and no questions are asked and no discussion ensues, then administrative decisions are "rubber stamped"; no "check and balance" exists.

The school board is supposed to act as the go-between for the school district and the community. That means that the community needs to be able to voice their concerns, address problems, and voice their desires to the board. The school district administrators and staff need to provide the school board with the facts. It is up to the board to drive policies and instruction by sorting out the details and giving direction to the district based on their combined educational philosophies. The three elements of the local education system—administration, the school board, and the people—are interconnected and barriers among the three in any form lead to dissatisfaction or dysfunction.

Recently, in a frustrated conversation with me over science education, one of my board members put it this way: "I'm an unpaid volunteer who doesn't understand the budget, has no expertise in the field of education; I don't have the answers to your questions and don't have the energy to chase them." This is an elected official who ran unopposed to represent the public. Does the public not know or not care or both?

Apathy and the "Me and Mine" Attitude of the Public

Apathy is a little difficult to discuss because of the potential for the misconception that understanding a concept equates to agreement, forgiveness, or tolerance of the situation. Apathy means "a lack of interest or indifference" (*Webster's*, 1976). It is certainly important for all of us to understand why and how so many people in our society display so much apathy.

Apathy is not directed just toward the school system. Look at our political system and this country's previous voting record compared to other democracies. We the people are supposed to serve as the ultimate check and balance through our power of the vote. But instead of being enthused about the democratic process or even being interested in the local control of schools, we find a very large number of people disconnected.

To understand this disconnect as it relates to schools, we have to think first about the people with the potential to be involved in the education system. We have those that care about all children, those that care only about their own children, and those that don't know enough to care. Some would argue that another very large group of people just don't and won't care. That group is lumped in with the group that doesn't know enough to care until proven otherwise.

It's easy to understand how a person who cares about all children can get caught up in the workings of a defective education system and become apathetic. If obvious mistakes are being made and you confront authority with facts, you risk being called "confrontational." If you critically evaluate a situation and let those findings be known, you are "nothing but critical." If the powers that be use the theory that they want their enemies close and place you on committee after committee, you run the risk of letting them "committee you to death."

When a person who gives of themselves for the betterment of all children sees things change for "the better" only to later see them change back to "the easier," you have to think about how much easier indifference would be to tolerate. When you work hard and long to change things only to realize that change doesn't last, that might make you give in to the easier path of apathy.

A couple of old sayings come to mind: "Accept the things you cannot change, change the things you can, and have the wisdom to know the difference." And, of course, "you can't change the system"; "you can't fight city hall." At this point, developing apathy may be the sanest thing to do. If you are a parent who cares about the children around you and knows that you have your own child in a dysfunctional school environment, you have to turn your concern towards your own child.

Caring about your own children and staying focused on and fighting for them is really what you are obligated to do as a good parent. If your attitude comes not from self-promotion but from the true need to survive a bad situation, no guilt should be felt about the focus of your efforts being on your child. But the "me and mine" attitude of the public makes it easy for administration and school boards to bulldoze over any single issue.

When parents or patrons see or hear of something that seems fundamentally wrong, as long as it doesn't affect them or their child, many of them aren't inclined to do too much about it just to defend a principle. This leaves individual parents with individual issues for any one administrator to handle. Administrators usually can easily defuse any single situation and go on their way to the next thing without "fixing" the root of any given problem. Do we really wonder why we continue to have problems?

The other aspect to consider when discussing apathy and the "me and mine" attitude of the public is the number of people that are ignorant about the inequality of our education system and the glaring problems occurring in many schools in the United States. They appear to be indifferent. They appear apathetic when, in fact, they may not know enough to care. Edwin E. Slosson in his book *The American Spirit in Education* stated this: "The very districts that needed good schools most were from their ignorance least conscious of the need" (1921, 107).

Ignorance can be overcome through knowledge. You can't expect people to be involved in their schools when they perceive that nothing needs to be done. No doubt, effective local control depends on an informed public. That is a problem, especially when we aren't even sure whose job it is to keep us informed about educational issues.

The movement to standards, testing, and the resultant No Child Left Behind law is a perfect example of what can happen when government moves ahead without the people understanding the intent and consequences of the law. That is how many government programs get put into place without the true informed consent of the people. If the people of the United States had understood the NCLB law before it was put in motion, they never would have approved; we wouldn't have spent so much money on testing and we wouldn't be looking at yet another change in the law. If we can't read it, understand it, and think it through before acting, maybe we shouldn't do it.

Historically, newspapers were seen as an essential vehicle for informing the public, for the public's voicing of opinions, and for opposing views. Today, they seem to instead interfere with the democratic process. Our local paper gives the impression that it is eager to avoid conflict with our city and school district and even more eager to voice the opinion of those entities and not necessarily the facts. Our local newspaper, along with our district, has failed to teach the public even the common educational language they need to know to understand the laws and in turn their rights. It has not been evident that the newspaper does any investigation into the facts. The reporters appear to be taking what they are told by our local administration to be true and digging no further for the facts. Public relations stories do not equal information; fluff does not equal facts.

So, as the years have passed, I continue to believe that school administration, school boards, and the public are the three problems at the heart of our education system's failures. When we begin to think of solutions, these problem areas all deserve to be put under the microscope. But certainly, in the perpetual flow of the system, major tributaries have contributed to the turbulence that has muddied the waters.

Curriculum and Testing

Curriculum is technically defined as "a fixed series of studies" (*Webster's*, 1976). Traditionally, the need to speak, write, read, and persuade drove the universal language curriculum elements. Our American predecessors also considered the concepts of mathematics and the ideas that belong to ethics and politics as essential. And nature study or the sciences were given importance in the schools of the past.

This all sounds easy; we should be able to set a fixed series of study down on paper. The problem is that what should be studied is not necessarily fixed. It varies based on the time, place, and needs of the local region, and let us not forget the needs and interests of the individual child. Possibly, if we had focused our efforts longer and harder on the standards and the curriculum that should have followed, we could have solved the age-old problem of what we, as a society in the United States of America, want our children to learn. Instead, we limited input from the public and dove into the testing aspect of education. And the dollars flowed in that direction.

What is the purpose of testing? The long-standing belief is that you use testing to find out what you know and don't know. It measures your knowledge. When testing takes place in a classroom situation, the test can be used by the student, with the help of the teacher, to pinpoint what the student may have misunderstood or failed to learn. The students can then go back and learn that information if they are so inclined.

The baffling thing is that somewhere along the way we have lost sight of that ideal. We aren't necessarily using tests that way; sometimes not even regular tests in the classroom. As previously mentioned, from about seventh grade on, not a single science test ever came home. Answer sheets with check marks and a grade arrived but without any indication what specific concept needed clarification.

It appears that the standard practice is for teachers to go through the test one time in class. That is probably fine for kids that don't miss many questions. But, if you have children who make many mistakes or have learning difficulties, asking them to grasp and remember all their mistakes during one review may be asking too much. Apparently the value in time spent contemplating and learning from mistakes has eluded many. Testing can become a barrier to learning rather than a tool for improvement.

The standards achievement tests deserve consideration as to whether they are of benefit or a barrier. Their purpose and use need to be scrutinized. When these tests first came out, no one seemed to know who was responsible for tracking a given child. A note might say that, based on test results, a child needed extra help, while the teacher handing it out might downplay that advice. That confuses parents.

In our district with its "failing" record, three months into the 2007 school year no one had asked for the supplemental services that were being offered as part of No Child Left Behind. Questions should be asked. The situation should have been a red flag as to inadequacies in public understanding of test results, how they should be related to learning, and what the NCLB law was put in place to do for children. In multiple ways, testing is not working how it was intended.

We don't have a single test that shows us how well our education system has prepared our children for life. Remember, how well we live life is the test. That's not to say that we vigilant people that care about the United States have no indicators of how well we are doing. The economy and our standing in the world on environmental, health, and other social issues including education are a few indicators among those to watch. The biggest question right now may very well be whether we are winning "the hearts and minds" war. You may think this is drifting off the subject of testing and the curriculum in alluding to the Iraq war and our wider-spread war on terror, but our global problems were actually predictable in some individuals' eyes.

In the 1956 book *A History of American Education*, author H. G. Good states: "There are some danger signs. One is the decline in the study of languages, mathematics, and the sciences. For economic development, for defense, for cooperation with our allies and the winning of new friends, these are important studies" (17). We are headed down a dangerous road when we narrow our curriculum to fit the test. Politics has taken us there.

Politics and Money

Which is worse: local politics or national politics? Or is politics just politics? Certainly the word itself leaves a bad taste in the mouths of many. The root of the word is "politic," which confusingly has two very different meanings. One is "having practical wisdom," while another is "unscrupulous" (*Webster's*, 1976) or unprincipled. Perhaps we should point the finger of blame at confusion.

Ideally, in our country, the public decides what it wants its young people to know and passes that information on to the school board, which sets the direction for the schools to be carried out by administration. Some of the questionable activities of our local school board, as previously described, illustrate one aspect of the downside of small town politics. A person's reason for seeking a board position and their reasoning behind the decisions they make should be questioned.

We voters don't always get many facts on which to base our decisions, forcing us to vote for or against whom we know or consider not voting at all. Rather than basing our vote on the beliefs of the candidate, many times personal rather than philosophical issues enter into the election of a local school board member. Or, in the case of an extremely apathetic public, one just needs to put their name in the hat to fill a vacated seat.

Our current local board has five members with only one that was originally seated in a regular election with an opponent. When something like this happens, no open discussion occurs concerning the desires and direction the board members wish to take. If no real candidates emerge, the philosophical direction your education board takes may never be revealed to the public. That is politics at its very worst, locally. On the state and national levels, education hasn't fared so well either.

The functions of state boards of education vary from state to state depending on state politics and policies and differing structures and functions of state administration. Our district is located in one of the most Republican states in the union. Our state legislature is dominated by Republicans with a Republican governor and a Republican state superintendent of schools, who is an elected official.

The direction of national education policy in the early 2000s has been dictated by a Republican president who passed major education legislation with a then-Republican Congress. If the No Child Left Behind law was going to work well, wouldn't you think it would be apparent here? It's their party.

That chiding of the Republican Party is just for amusement; the reality is that throughout history it really hasn't mattered which party set the direction of the education plan. It is the surest bet that a plan will fail to fulfill its goal. In part this is due to the fact that the plan changes every four to eight years with the election of a new president.

President Johnson's 1965 education law was aimed at "educationally deprived children" with funding appropriations that were never fulfilled. The first President Bush set goals for the "America 2000" program; President Clinton gave us "Principles of Effectiveness," while the second President Bush gave us "No Child Left Behind." You would think that the U.S. Congress would try to hold things steady. Many of them have been holding a seat for twenty or more years.

It really should not surprise us that these long-standing representatives have failed to adequately represent our children. They are so far removed personally from the education system; they may not realize what is going on. They just govern it! Do you think we might be at the point yet where we consider that it is time to quit allowing the children of the United States to be used as pawns in the political games being played out from Washington, D.C., to our local districts?

Technically, education is a responsibility of each state, but realistically we should be facing the fact that our decisions are being restricted and directed by the federal government. They, like our local and state governments, don't seem to understand that success has more to do with the implementation of a plan than the plan itself. Being at the mercy of political whims, it should be no surprise that we are looking at the same problems in education that we have been trying to solve throughout the history of education in the United States. Except now the money connection is stronger than ever.

Education is big business. Among the common people, it is a widely accepted view that our political system is directed more by money than the desires of the people. The result of that is that we are letting politics and money set our educational philosophy. No Child Left Behind, once again, can be used as an example.

NCLB forced us to collectively and separately spend billions on development and testing of tests. Individuals then spend countless dollars on what can be called the "cottage industries" of education. These are all the businesses that have sprung up to help children pass the tests and also to fill our system's educational gaps. If parents know enough to be concerned about their child's education or test scores and they find they aren't getting help or cooperation from the public education system, they can turn to tutoring or publications for help—if it is something they can afford.

By the very nature of the funding for NCLB, it leaves children behind. In particular, it is leaving behind those that are getting their last chance to make their diploma mean something, our high school students. They are worth mentioning again as is the money trail.

Funding is based on formulas, and, in districts such as mine, we reached the maximum allotted for Title 1 schools, meaning low-income schools, and are forced to decide where to best use those funds. It has become common, recommended practice to use fewer of these dollars at the high school level because the students' test scores only count once for NCLB in grades 9–12.

In other words, the children at our high school were eligible for funds because of the high poverty rate, but the government emphasis has directed schools to put their money into the earlier grades, resulting in what amounts to turning their backs on the failing high school students, giving them their diplomas and sending them into the world.

Look at the money trail of No Child Left Behind. Look into the eyes of the failing high school students that are left with the crumbs of a remedial program because the money was directed to the lower grades and tell them they aren't being left behind. Look them in the eyes and explain how the money is better spent in the early years. Tell them what the research shows. And tell them that No Child Left Behind isn't just a slogan.

But the money trail and its political connections don't stop at this point. When your schools fail to make adequate yearly progress, the law tells you that you may have to fully implement a new curriculum. Your district may be led to believe that it has to buy into a research-based "program" to fix its problem. Companies that have gotten their programs on the right list have done well.

NCLB directives have pushed districts toward investing in programs rather than developing their own teaching philosophies to fit their needs. That is still not the end of the money trail with NCLB. When it talks about turning over schools to private companies with "a demonstrated record of effectiveness," we need to really be looking hard at educational research.

Research vs. Reality

Educational research has fascinated and baffled me. A scientist thinking about research thinks about holding all variables constant in an experiment except the one being tested; that is impossible in the education system. Educational research deals with individual little people and their attached individual families. Variables are plentiful. That was the baffling part for me.

The fascinating part was coming to the realization that research can also be defined as "careful study and investigation to discover or establish facts or principles" (*Webster's*, 1976). Put in that context, research in education is much more open to interpretation so it's much less absolute than pure scientific research, if such a thing as absolute or pure exists. Yet, time and again, administrators and others defend their position on an issue based totally on what the research shows. Educational research has to be taken with a grain of salt just given its very nature. It's not the same as scientific research in other fields. In education more often it's about correlations rather than establishing a cause and effect relationship.

The flaw in relying strictly on research, and therefore our often misdirected efforts, can best be explained by again making a comparison to the practice of medicine. Practicing medicine is not a pure science. Scientific facts are used as guides but, when dealing with a living thing, variables are going to change your expected outcome. These are things we have no control over. Each living being is unique. That's the reality. That

CHAPTER 5

is why the "practice" of medicine is referred to as "an art and a science." In the practice of good quality medicine, prevention of medical problems and response to any necessary treatment should always be gauged on an individual basis. In the education setting, the people that are best able to judge the condition of a student are the ones the children see daily—their teachers and parents.

Liberty and Listening

Teachers and parents are the groups you would hope to be hearing the most from when discussing improvements in education. They are the ones most intimately connected to the education system through children on a day-to-day basis. You would think their input and feedback would not only be welcomed but recognized as essential to a quick response when a problem is sensed.

Unfortunately, these two groups are the ones most afraid of the repercussions of expressing dissatisfaction, concerns, or reservations over a whole host of issues at multiple levels. Some parents fear that what they say may lead to more difficult times for their children. It happens. They don't want to risk it. Some teachers fear reprimands or fear for their jobs. That happens, too. Overridden by fear, these groups are keeping their opinions to themselves. They are giving up their voice in the decision-making process. The very people that the system should be responding to in order for continued improvement to occur are the ones feeling least at liberty to speak.

Teachers are being arbitrarily controlled by inflexible or overbearing administrators. Even worse, they are being controlled by the government through testing results. Parents are being controlled from multiple directions including by administrators, teachers, and coaches. This suggests that we have decided to give up a piece of our liberty. Liberty means "freedom from any form of arbitrary control" (*Webster's*, 1976). Here in the United States, we are supposed to be at liberty to use our freedom of speech. It's not working well in the bureaucracy we call the education system.

Fortunately, some teachers and parents exist as exceptions. They are the individuals that "buck the system" or, in some people's analysis, are just plain critical and cause problems. Thank goodness for them, because they are the ones that keep poorly performing schools from totally falling apart.

These are the people that some would laughingly refer to as "watch dogs." These brave individuals make noise, but is anyone really listening?

Listening skills appear to be something that fewer and fewer people possess. Not too long ago a magazine wrote about things that other countries do better than we do in the United States. One of those things was the art of conversation. That should be no surprise.

To converse, you have to patiently listen, really listen, before responding. In our hurry-up world we are modeling ineffective communication skills to the next generation. We also have people that know how to listen but make the choice not to listen. So, in the bigger picture on the subjects of liberty and listening, think about how it doesn't take decisions being made behind closed doors to kill a democracy; for those in power to destroy this republic, all they need to do is quit listening to the people.

If you have been listening to discussions about education, it has become fairly common to hear folks voicing the opinion that the blame rests on the shoulders of the teachers, parents, and kids. Many would argue that teachers, parents, and students are the whole problem. These people must consider and understand that the system has failed time and again to train and retrain educators properly, it has failed to inform parents of their role in the task of educating, and it is mismanaging too many students to hold them accountable.

The system has failed to thoroughly educate the public about educational issues. It has failed to show understanding of the learning environment that needs to be created in classrooms to provide what children need to best learn. Along with the Big Three (administration, the school board, and the public), the bureaucracy full of educated, credentialed, well-paid personnel and politicians is also at the root of the problem.

I don't see teachers, parents, and kids as the problem; they are a large part of the solution.

CHAPTER SIX
WE HAVE THE ANSWERS

Ask Counsel of both Times: of the Ancient Time, what of it is worth keeping, and of the Latter Time, what is fittest for the new day; but seek as well to create Good Precedents as to follow them.

Francis Bacon

At one frustrating moment in time, the thought occurred to me that providing equal opportunity to a good quality education was too complicated a proposition to ever achieve. Now, through observation, inquiry, and research, the facts are very clear that the "fixes" are laid out before us; they have been for a long time. They have surfaced and are within our grasps. The question is: Will we pull them from the stream or watch them once more float away, go under, only to resurface again in the future, too late for us?

H. G. Good made the observation: "American education has been brought down from the clouds to deal with the needs of the office, farm, mart, shop, and home, where people work and live. This is good precedent. But the problems of philosophy, government, and pure science are not therefore to be less studied" (1956, v).

This statement implies that, in looking at providing a quality education to all children, we must be looking at our needs while keeping the idea of balance in mind. To achieve balance, you wouldn't jump from one side to another. You wouldn't pull one thing off or shove on another. You wouldn't make any sudden or radical moves. You would sense your imbalance, adjust accordingly, and attempt to inch your way to success.

Safe and Disciplined Schools

> The teacher should find the cause of misconduct and should treat that
> rather than the symptoms.
>
> Christopher Dock

Christopher Dock's statement should not be misconstrued, when applied
to our modern times, to mean that the teacher is solely responsible for the
cure of students' misconduct. It should be looked at from the perspective
that when children intentionally misbehave, they may very well be indicating that something is amiss in their lives or in the immediate learning
environment. The "bad" behavior should first be considered a symptom,
not an indication that the child is "bad." We need to continually be solving
the discipline problems in our classrooms so that we can ensure instruction without interruption. The solution to the tough issue of creating
disciplined classrooms lies in the ideals of creating safe school environments. That means beginning with understanding the causes behind the
symptoms.

Having spent years listening to discussions about the issues surrounding safe schools, the fact is that collectively we know and have a good understanding of most of the causes of misconduct and the prevention and
interventions that are effective. In *Hope Fulfilled for At-Risk and Violent
Youth: K–12 Programs That Work*, Robert Barr and William Parrett claim:
"We now know beyond a shadow of doubt that all children can learn,
that effective schools can overcome the debilitating effects of poverty
and dysfunctional families, and we know exactly what schools must do to
accomplish this reality. What remains is the collective will to act" (2001,
xii). Another author, Peter Sacks, opens his book, *Standardized Minds:
The High Price of America's Testing Culture and What We Can Do to Change
It*, by stating, "In my research for this book, I was struck by a profound
disconnection between knowledge and practice" (1999, xi). Sacks, Barr,
and Parrett are experts in their chosen areas who live in my state. They are
homegrown experts, so to speak, but they, their work, and their findings
are unknown to my community. Their voice has been missing.

Teachers, administrators, parents, and the greater community need
to make better use of the existing body of expertise and their available
community resources. We need to put the knowledge we've accumulated

into practice. The solution to schools that struggle could quickly begin to take form if we combine the efforts of already existing school personnel positions and resources already in place to help our youth. Through a community position designed to coordinate the multiple government bureaucracies and private youth foundations and institutions, we can bring knowledge into the hands of those that can use it and resources to the feet of the children that so desperately need it. That is the one idea that I call my own and, for this discussion, I refer to the position as a community education coordinator.

Existing in our education system are federal, state, and school coordinator positions referred to as safe and drug-free schools coordinators. "Drug-free" has been lumped together with "safe schools" in that title and job description. We need drug education. It is an assumption that it is part of school curricula. But we need to remove the "drug-free" wording and emphasis from these positions, not because we should remove drug education, but because we need to fight our human nature to do the easier thing. It is easier to focus on the drug education piece when you are a safe and drug-free schools coordinator than to tackle safe and disciplined school issues. If these positions were only focused on safe schools issues, these school coordinators would quickly come to the same conclusion many others did years ago.

Safety and discipline are community issues. These are issues of establishing civility on our streets and in our classrooms. This is about establishing socially accepted behavior. Communities need to set their expectations, make those expectations known, work together to meet them, and constantly remind each other that we are to model them in all aspects of our public lives. Adults need to support each other in this endeavor. Teachers and parents need to communicate expectations of behavior and share experiences freely back and forth. Parents need to know how they can help the teachers, and teachers need to know where they can find help when things aren't going as expected.

Creating safe schools that are conducive to respectful attitudes and self-discipline can't be treated like just any other job in the school setting. Safe and disciplined schools issues deserve attention in and of themselves and the problems that our young people are bringing to school with them can't be solved strictly within the institutional walls of a school. They are the ultimate community issue and must be approached at that level. That is best done by coordinating the efforts inside the school with those out in the community.

Successful programs or attempts to address issues related to discipline, community improvement, and the resultant school improvement appear to have several elements in common. They include bringing caring community members together, assessing the needs of the community, setting goals, assessing the effective services available, targeting unmet needs, and assessing the results against their goals. These steps are done on an ongoing basis and goals are adjusted as indicated by the needs identified within a given community. Communities have paid consultants to come in and conduct these types of programs. Others have done it themselves seeming to unknowingly follow the same logical steps as others before them, or have been fortunate enough to work with an organization set up to do this very thing.

One element that is essential to success in these communities seeking to improve themselves and their school systems is the ability to communicate facts, ideas, goals, and expectations to the schools and the general public alike. Communication is essential to helping ensure the success and sustainability of any community plan.

A community education coordinator position may first be used to function as a catalyst to stimulate interest in the improvement process. Developing within people the will to act is more often challenging than not. An understanding of the change process is essential. These are concepts that could and should be brought to a community in depth.

Briefly, in the early 1900s, Edward L. Thorndike was credited with defining education as the production of change in people. Much later, the Concerns-Based Adoption Model set the stage for new teacher professional development models based on the philosophies outlined by Susan Loucks-Horsley (1996). Her working theory emphasizes that education leads to change. Change brings different levels of concerns to people. Those concerns need to be addressed in order for them to progress to the action phase.

In addition, we need to reconsider the theory of action developed by the National Science Resource Center. That model emphasized that, as your basis for change, you have research findings upon which you develop a shared vision for your community. Common sense and research both tell us that a plan has a better chance of succeeding when those that must carry it out have a say in it. These models should and could be applied to safe schools issues.

It should become apparent that bringing knowledge of research to community members, using the research to develop a vision, and moving a community into action take coordination. And the communication, necessary to make this happen, needs to be of both the research on which a vision should be developed and the developed vision.

The goal of a community education coordinator, in this case, can be seen as similar to that of the original American Lyceum. The American Lyceum was founded in 1826 by Josiah Holbrook. It was a system of adult education that used lectures, debates, and readings to reach out to the public with the goal of disseminating information for the betterment of community schools. The lyceum was dedicated "to procure for youths an economical and practical education and to diffuse rational and useful information through the community generally" (*Encyclopedia Americana*, 1999, vol. 17, 878). The official organization died shortly after the Civil War. The precursor to the original American Lyceum is considered to be the Junto, which was established by Benjamin Franklin and was where books were shared and ideas debated. In turn, the lyceum is given credit for being the basis of the idea behind the current university extension system.

I tend to believe that, had the lyceum stayed in existence and brought current information to our community on safety and discipline issues in 1999, many of the problems associated with our gangs and general delinquent behaviors, and the resultant classroom disruptions, could have been alleviated. A community education coordinator could now serve to facilitate bringing pertinent up-to-date information to foster improvements in school climates. It is a function that could serve a variety of community topics from health issues to energy usage and would reasonably include academics.

The Three Rs

One-fourth of the students who applied for college admissions around 1862 did not have "a good common school education" and the colleges found it necessary to establish preparatory departments. . . . This also has bearing upon the present controversy over the past and present effectiveness of the schools in teaching the Three R's.

H. G. Good

We need to look at both the past and the present debates about teaching the Three Rs. The optimist wants to say that we are doing a better job in many ways, while the realist is still seeing twenty-eight children in first grade classes without the help needed to attend to individual learning needs. The realist still sees children leaving first grade without the skills they need to sufficiently progress. The optimist thinks we will learn from the past, this time.

It seems that the debate on how to teach reading, writing, and arithmetic has been raging since the beginning of U.S. history. In the early years of our country, before it was ours, our schools were modeled after those of the countries of origin of the people who settled a particular area. The teaching methods of different regions followed the teaching philosophies brought over by immigrants. Between the settlers spending their time concentrating on the necessities of life, working on establishing a new country, the influx of different people with varied philosophies, and the intermittent general public neglect of the importance of education and its funding, the United States has lost its philosophical footing repeatedly when it comes to teaching the Three Rs.

The importance of understanding the philosophy behind our decisions about education is something that has escaped many. Some have openly asked why the teaching philosophies are deemed so important to a discussion. That is a good sign; that opens up discussion further. Others miss the importance of it totally, as was unmistakable when a school board member openly scoffed at the idea of spending time discussing the philosophy behind a policy before proceeding. This occurred while serving on the policy committee. That's a bad sign—expressing your philosophy can be seen as an effort to make your general ideas clear. It serves to help us define our goals or objectives. In policies, it should help us ensure that our objectives are clear. In turn, what you teach and how you teach depends on your goals, which should be based on your philosophies.

Philosophy is also defined as "a particular system of principles for the conduct of life" or can be used to describe "a treatise covering such a system" (*Webster's*, 1976). It should serve as a guide. Another way of looking at the importance of philosophy in education is to look at how it presents itself in the reality of the school setting. For example, when you see only whole language being used to teach reading, as a parent, you should consider asking the district about its teaching philosophy toward phonics.

Since most parents are currently not a part of guiding their school's curriculum and instruction, understanding what beliefs your district bases its decisions on is useful in lending some consistency to your child's education and is helpful in more quickly detecting deficits or glaring differences with your own beliefs.

To bring the idea of the importance of philosophy full circle, we need to ask the universities and colleges that produce our teachers: Are they preparing teachers to follow the teaching philosophies and principles that we in the United States believe to be the direction we wish to take? Do you know what our U.S. teaching philosophies and principles are? Based on many years of research and experimentation what have we, as a people, decided are the principles on which we wish to effectively teach the Three Rs? This is not the same as asking about national standards or a national curriculum. This is asking for clarification about what we believe works best in teaching the Three Rs. It has become clear that we no longer seem to believe in mastery before promotion. But, as just a parent, the systems guiding principles have not been and are still not clear.

Throughout the years, it seems that the philosophies have changed many times over in keeping with the latest educational fads, often swinging dramatically from one side of the belief spectrum to the other. Historically, that is also true but recurrent themes throughout the history of American education seem evident. Many of those recurrent ideals look to be good starting points, excellent middle ground upon which we could build understanding of what we as a nation value in education.

In talking about colonial Americans and their lack of knowledge about the science of language, H. G. Good concluded that "their greatest mistake was the failure to understand that speech is the real, the living language and that writing and print are only its lifeless symbols" (1956, 33). Many much-admired men in the field of education believed that drawing should come before writing and the art of conversation before reading. As mentioned previously, the art of conversation in the United States is waning. With this next generation growing up with the technological substitutes for human interaction that they have available, we might want to pay close attention to focusing on the elements of conversation: thinking, speaking, listening, and questioning.

Conversation is not a focus of the No Child Left Behind law. Reading is and does deserve the spotlight. It appears that our brush with success in reading instruction occurred back in Delaware around 1640, as described by Edwin E. Slosson. Slosson explains how the Swedes had settled that area and at the time it was said that "there was not a peasant child in Sweden who had not been taught to read and write" (1921, 38). However, as this segment of the colony became incorporated into a more diverse community, its "education left no traceable mark on the later educational history of Delaware" (39).

We have ignored the teaching successes of other countries as well, including the Germans, who have consistently been teaching reading through a combination of word and phonics methods. The belief is that we are doing this now, again, also. The belief is that we have found a balance between using word and phonetic instruction. Is that our current philosophy about reading instruction? Is that just the latest trend or do our oversights ensure it continues? And what is our philosophy on writing instruction?

Writing has two elements to it that deserve particular attention: the mechanical part that is of course not necessarily tested on NCLB and the grammatical part that is tested to some extent. With well-established mandatory testing, we shouldn't have to worry about sentence structure not being taught. What we as a nation should be discussing is the importance of writing itself. An emphasis on writing has been shown to be a common factor among high-achieving schools. Writing is not just grammar lessons that can be tested by multiple choice questions. It requires multiple thought processes that train the brain in a way very different from memorizing word patterns. And the mechanics of cursive are just now being associated with the ability to take quick and accurate notes. How important is that to us?

The same question should be asked about spelling. As mentioned previously, spelling is very important in many workplaces. When you receive a written message that you cannot decipher due to words you don't recognize, it's a problem. Workplace efficiency decreases. When that same issue arises in medical records, the problem becomes potentially dangerous.

Frustration with the inventive spelling concept is one thing; its potential detriment to society is another. How we teach spelling deserves more consideration. Using spelling lists and tests to "drill and kill" is not the only way to accomplish the task of producing adequate spellers. Spelling can be taught differently if we decide to approach it with a different philosophy.

History provides another option to consider; it is that you learn to spell words correctly as you use them. It has been suggested that the schools create a correct-spelling habit and correct-spelling conscience. That means we need to provide multiple opportunities for children to write, opportunities that need to span the length of their K–12 careers. Providing those opportunities requires that time is allowed for those activities in the curriculum. With only so much time in a school day, it seems that knowing what we citizens value and agreeing on teaching philosophies would be helpful in making decisions on how best to have our children spend their time. That same idea should be applied to arithmetic instruction.

Math has gone the way of multiple directions of emphasis. An interesting concept was one developed around 1900 called the "social use principle," which used as its guide to teaching those things that had "a clear link to usefulness in life." In one investigation, a survey was done on arithmetic concepts and practices needed in occupations: "Everybody agreed that pupils should learn to perform the four fundamental operations with whole numbers and small fractions, confidently, rapidly, and accurately; and that they should be taught to check their results" (Good, 416). People in various occupations would wholeheartedly agree with that assessment of needed math skills.

From store-owners to medical professionals, when you no longer have confidence in your staff to do the math correctly, you do it yourself, taking away time from your work and decreasing your efficiency. Having our graduates able to do basic math is a reasonable expectation for our education system to deliver. Many other math skills are relevant but people have not agreed upon their importance. Those discussions need to continue and we must decide the question of how to teach.

Balance between philosophies would serve us well. To balance the conceptual with the practical, we need both hands-on manipulation of learning materials to solidify concepts and rote memorization of math facts to ensure the desired accuracy. Is that the philosophy behind which we wish to develop our instruction?

In the words of a teacher whose opinion I value, I quote: "In fact, the quality of instruction and assessment may decline as teachers are forced to value what is measured instead of measuring what we value." Who is deciding what we value?

CHAPTER 6

Science Education

> The greatest deficiency of the teachers lay in the lack of a thorough scientific education. It is a great mistake to suppose that just any one can teach even the simple elements of science. To have a smattering of something is one of the greatest fallacies of our time.
>
> Edward Austin Sheldon

Many of our children are only receiving a smattering of science education. This is a result of allowing wide variation between the states in the emphasis on what subject matter we consider important enough to teach in the United States. With the lip service given to the importance of math and science, particularly as it applies to the economy, you wouldn't think making a case for teaching science would be needed. The fact is that the need is huge.

To begin with, we have different definitions of science. The hope would be that we could all agree that the study of science should include knowledge of nature and the physical world plus an understanding of the principles and methods of scientific study. To understand those principles and methods, critical thinking skills become essential.

Critical thinking skills require careful analysis, good judgment, and the ability to ask good questions and seek their answers. For children to understand science, they need to observe accurately and master the principles of science, not just cover what's in the book to later regurgitate facts on a test. Mastering principles requires the time to question the "facts." The education system needs to understand that concept and they need to learn to nurture a child's natural curiosity—not kill it.

Children learn instinctively through all their given senses. They feel, taste, smell, hear, and see the world around them. They imitate the people about them, learning by example. As they grow, if allowed, they question all that surrounds them. That is inquiry-based learning; that is hands-on learning. For thousands of years, we humans have understood that concept. Aristotle has been quoted as saying "Nothing is in the mind that is not first in the hand." Is the educational community listening? What we really need to understand from history is why it has been so hard to keep quality science education in the elementary schools.

A couple of things need to be clarified before proceeding. First, some of you may be questioning the necessity of science education in the earlier grades. Probably the two best arguments in favor of elementary science education are that (1) a student needs many years in order to allow complex science concepts to become solid thoughts, and (2) quality science instruction incorporates reading, writing, and mathematics, and provides hands-on, inquiry-centered learning to add relevance, stimulate interest, and in turn increase a student's effort in active learning. That is a philosophy we should consider establishing.

Second, many of you may be assuming that science has been and is taught in the elementary grades. For some districts, that may be true; for others, it is not. A smidgen at this age doesn't count as quality. For example, our district has taken the Open Court reading program and aligned reading of science facts to the science standards. Teachers that understand and love teaching science find ways to supplement those lessons with hands-on materials. Experiences of the past tell us that it won't be consistent. Whether a single child receives quality science instruction throughout the primary and secondary school years is left up to luck.

If people realized how important it is for children to learn an adequate amount of quality science, they wouldn't be leaving that opportunity up to luck. The importance of science education is obviously being misunderstood. We can fix that.

Many citizens of the United States have been talking about the need for more able scientists for many, many years. Corporations, institutions, and professions are considering, or already are, importing more scientists or outsourcing where that is possible. And technology is making more things possible. Many of these jobs are good jobs that our students, being unprepared, don't even consider. We can change that.

But the goal is not to make everyone a scientist. We need to develop citizens able to understand the complex issues of our society today, many of which are based in one branch of science or another. That is what you hear referred to as "scientific literacy." It means we want everyone to have the science background they need to function well in our society. We must accomplish that.

We must decide what we value. We need to hear open, widespread public discussion about the state of science education and what we should be doing as a nation.

Historically, the problems associated with sustaining science education in the elementary schools have included: inadequate scientific education of the elementary teachers which leads to decreased enthusiasm for teaching it, heavy schedules, large class sizes, lack of administrative support, and inadequate supply of tasks and materials to do hands-on science. It sounds like an all-encompassing list of problems in a chapter devoted to solutions.

There is not one item on that list for which one of the richest, most powerful countries on the planet can't provide, if we so desired.

Other Desirable Subjects

> The education of the many in the practical affairs of life is no substitute for the cultivation of high genius for mathematics, physics, chemistry; and it is also dangerous to neglect the humanities—for what shall it profit a man to save his life and lose his sense of values?
>
> H. G. Good

That you found no chapters devoted to social studies, humanities, or the arts is not because of viewing them as lesser subjects. They definitely are not less significant than the Three Rs and science. These subjects are many times seen as "other" but should be considered desirable and deserving of their rightful place in all school curricula. We should not neglect their careful, thoughtful consideration in our system.

Edwin Slosson talked about Benjamin Franklin's theories on mental and moral education. He discussed Franklin's desires for the teaching of history: "It is universal and comparative history that he wants, with special reference to customs, politics, religion, natural resources, commerce, and the growth of science. History, thus properly taught, would naturally lead to the study of ethics, logic, physics, oratory, debating, and journalism" (1921, 70). Benjamin Franklin was a man who knew through experience what it took to be an inventor and a fine statesman; this was a man who embodied the American spirit of resourcefulness and initiative. We should listen and contemplate his, as well as others', ideals concerning education.

Others have talked about the need to first teach history about your local region and visit local historical sights to connect kids to the history in their own backyards, thus stimulating interest in the subject to further a student's effort to study and learn. Still others in the past have discussed ways of expanding the subjects we teach without taking anything away from the teaching of the Three Rs.

That ideal can become reality only after we come to a decision to: set our focus on clarifying what we value in education; quit wasting time changing gears with every new educational fad; and bring stability, balance, and fairness to the governing philosophy of our system.

The Big Three in Education

> School people are to the last degree impatient of criticism and suggestion. They resent them as a reflection on their personal character. As one man, they rush to the defense. The better among them excuse the worst and the worst grow abusive.
>
> Nicholas Murray Butler

Over the years, when thinking about how to address the problems created by the Big Three in education (administration, the school board, and the public), no solutions or ways to change the system could be found. Trying to analyze the problems would draw you into a never-ending circle of thought. It felt like being caught up in a whirlpool.

After much effort to break free of the vicious cycle of thoughts, some reasonable conclusions were made that could be deemed helpful: the administration should at least know the basic research findings on any issue before making a decision; the school board members should begin by reviewing their state code governing education and their own code of ethics in order to function; and the teachers and parents must unite to stimulate interest in education within the general public.

They aren't bad suggestions, but they do demonstrate our tendency to want to dissect the problem. We want to break up our problems into small pieces that we feel are doable. It's what scientists tend to do. It's the way government bureaucracies are set up, in divisions. But, in doing so, we continue to fail to fix the bigger problem, the bigger picture. Something is always missing.

On August 15, 2007, the day the writing of this book began, the intention was to offer the idea of the community education coordinator position as the answer to help correct the failures witnessed under this local control system. Local control does not work 100 percent of the time.

Indications are that it is not coming close. Its inability to work resulted in our school district's failings—no question. The Big Three must share some of the blame. They must become part of the solution.

A community education coordinator working through already existing education agencies could help a local school board achieve the function for which it was intended. A community education coordinator could function to help educate the public and stimulate the needed interest in education. That position could be used to foster the development of the essential intimate, barrier-free relationship of the community and school. It could promote the cooperation necessary to encourage us to listen to one another.

But what I now doubt is whether or not this type of reform would be enough. I, like Seymour Sarason and others, question the existing structure that currently governs education, from top to bottom. The Big Three have been so strongly influenced by state, federal, and local politics that, alone, they may never break free of that authority and obtain the liberty to pursue the right course for education.

Formula for Success

> Let us think of education as the means of developing our greatest abilities, because in each of us there is a private hope and dream which, fulfilled, can be translated into benefit for everyone and greater strength for our nation.
>
> John F. Kennedy

When considering the complex interrelationships and the entrenchment of the parties involved in education, to break free of this whirlpool of thoughts, we must focus on the nuts and bolts of what is right. To think through this concept of universal public education, the essential elements of education are easiest to look at and think about in the form of an equation. If we, as a nation, focus and stay focused long enough, we can work through this equation. My hope is that this formula provides clarity to those of you whose vision has been clouded by the complexities of the politics of education, is used to refocus our thoughts during times of confusion, and focuses our actions.

We have made this whole business of educating children way too complicated. The resulting costs to run this bureaucracy that we have developed have been detrimental to the education of the children that it was supposed to serve.

The basic formula is:

Kids Ready to Learn	+	Teachers Ready to Teach	+	The Materials to Do It	=	Equal Opportunity for Education

Kids Ready to Learn
The secret of right education consists in respecting the pupil.

Ralph Waldo Emerson

When we think about kids coming to school ready to learn, multiple things come to mind. Do they get enough sleep? Are they hungry? Are they emotionally ready to learn? Do they live in a nurturing environment? Do they have a home? The recipe for "Kids Ready to Learn" is a long and varied one.

Should the American government and the schools be responsible to ensure all the factors necessary for having kids ready to learn are in place? Of course they shouldn't, and they can't. It is up to parents and the communities in which they live. It is a community issue. But the larger education system and the schools can do more to help the community address these issues. They can begin by clearly defining and making known their expectations.

Ruby Payne stresses the importance of support, insistence, and expectations in her book titled *Working with Parents: Building Relationships for Student Success* (2005). Her experiences communicating with the different economic class cultures point out the importance of understanding how to communicate with the group you are trying to reach and the importance of clarifying your expectations. Dr. Payne explains that the "societal rules" are different depending upon which economic class you experienced in childhood. We can't expect or take for granted that everyone follows or even understands the rules by which we govern schools. She states that, for many children raised in poverty, "schools are virtually the only places where students can learn the choices and rules of the middle class" (62).

We really do need to explain our expectations of behaviors for the child and the expectations of the parental role. We shouldn't take for granted that everyone has the same meaning for even the word "respect." We need to teach and reteach our behavioral expectations in an ongoing and developmentally appropriate manner to the children and in an economic-class appropriate manner to the parents and the community in general. And all people need to model those behaviors.

In a book called *Central Park East and Its Graduates: "Learning by Heart,"* David Bensman describes the investigation he conducted through interviews of the students and their parents years after the kids had graduated from this elementary school. One of the key things he contributed to this school being successful (as judged by notably high graduation rates, college acceptance rates, and personal satisfaction of its graduates) was the consistent respect shown for children, parents, and teachers.

Bensman also noted that time and again former students would tell him that they felt supported and encouraged. They also felt that, among other things, they came away from this school understanding the ideal of "respect for the human spirit's creativity and the American citizen's communal responsibility" (2000, 8). And one of his conclusions was that "children quickly learned that their family and school were of one mind not only about the importance of learning, but about what children had to do to learn" (103).

Children are so easily influenced. So, let's not blame the students. When children come to school unprepared to learn, many times it is because they don't know how to behave; it is not the fault of the child. But too many times they are the ones that ultimately suffer. It is very sad to watch children arrive at school full of excitement, curiosity, and enthusiasm and be "put down" because they haven't been taught how to behave. Too many times we forget about the feelings of the child because we have to get on to the lesson. We forget that respect for each other is central to how we treat each other. It is always a two-way street.

As mentioned previously, one definition of "discipline" is that it is the process of training a child so that the desired character traits and habits can be developed. It isn't a matter of domination or strict "classroom control"; it's the development of personal character traits that act to serve our students well throughout life. Those desired traits and habits need to be defined and communicated so they can be modeled at home and in the community and need only reinforcement in the schools. This process requires much more than just listing what we want to see developed, handing it out, or mailing it home. It requires open discussion about what works, what doesn't, and what we as a community can do short term and long term to accomplish what we desire.

We need to coordinate the effort to work with educators and the public on developing their message of expectations and getting it out to the community through existing adult education agencies. The basics of any issue are not so complicated that everyday people can't understand them. Put into a variety of media forms using language that people can understand, we can get our messages through to the people that need them. That builds consistency.

Inconsistency leads to confusion and frustration on the part of the child. Frustration can lead to violence. That is not conducive to having them ready to learn. For that reason, it is important that in addition to the schools making known their expectations, parents must be able to discuss the expectations they have of the school. The school does have other roles in helping children to be ready to learn.

The schools should not fail to provide children with the essentials for learning or fail to reinforce lessons that good parents try to instill in their children. To be ready to learn, children need access to water, bathroom facilities, proper nutrition, fresh air periodically, and recreational exercise (particularly for the very young learners) to help facilitate a fresh view on learning. If parents value fairness, acceptance of others' views, and the development of good study habits, schools should reinforce those values.

Children getting mixed signals are confused, not ready to learn. That makes the job for parents more difficult; it makes the teachers' job more difficult. Open discussion of our expectations of each other would go a long way in preventing difficulties.

It is the responsibility of parents to take care of their own children and prepare them for their place in the community. It is not the responsibility of our government. But the reality is that many do not or cannot do this, at this point in time, to meet the demands of our rapidly changing society. Our economy and our changing values have been detrimental to the family unit; that is a fact, not a pass.

There is no excusing the fact that too many parents have not made educating their children a priority, or made their children in any way their number one priority, period. This has gotten us into a vicious cycle that we must break. Education is the vehicle through which we can. We need to begin with educating our families on how best to get the next generation ready for its opportunity for a better education. Our government holds some responsibility for that achievement. Key to our success is parental education.

What children need to be ready to learn should not be seen as a discussion about just early childhood education. Parent education topics need to be seen as a spectrum that addresses the issues that the teachers are seeing in the classrooms. While the sleepy first graders' parents may need to know about sleep requirements for that age, the "zoned-out" teenagers may need sex education so they can put their emotions in check and get back to learning.

As communities, we can do a better job getting our children ready to learn so that our teachers can carry on with their jobs. Some "business-minded models" have been looking at the "economy of time" as it relates to the classroom. They would be wise to pause a moment, look back at the work of their predecessors, and then consider anew how we can best make more time for teaching. If children don't become major distractions in the classroom setting, don't teachers have more time to teach?

Teachers Ready to Teach

Teacher and child are the leading characters in the educational drama. If the child is to play his part well, the teacher should be well prepared.

H. G. Good

Teaching became a profession during the middle 1800s. The criteria upon which it gained status as a profession were that the need for special preparation was recognized and developed. Thus, teachers became recognized professionals. "Professionals" are defined as "engaged in or worthy of the high standards of a profession" (*Webster's*, 1976).

Having no formal training in the field of education, I don't claim and won't pretend to know what aspects and elements of the teaching process are included in teacher preparation. What can be claimed is that I have been through training for a profession; I too am labeled a professional. Before entering the profession of veterinary medicine, the expectations of the profession and the concept of "standards of practice" were made very clear and those same ideals reinforced repeatedly throughout the preparation process and through continuing education. A consistent message about maintaining a standard was upheld.

As any professional knows, maintaining high standards requires constant vigilance on an individual's part to keep up with current information and practices. As a professional, it is that person's responsibility to maintain high standards. That is what professionals do.

But it appears that what differs greatly between my profession and teaching is that in the veterinary medical profession across the country, we have a clearer, more consistent teaching curriculum that our universities follow in our instruction. The knowledge of the sciences, practices, and procedures that veterinarians receive is reliable. Our preparation and continuing education is based on what we need to know to practice the art and science of veterinary medicine successfully. Success depends on our guiding beliefs.

In the art and science of teaching, that does not appear to be the case. It has not been obvious what the prevailing educational philosophies are that we taught and are teaching to teachers, counselors, and administrators. If society hasn't decided the prevailing direction of instruction, how can we possibly know what to teach our teachers? Experience points to the fact that, with such change and variation in methods, instruction, and emphasis of subjects (or lack thereof), it is difficult to know how colleges and universities are setting their aim on what to teach to teachers.

It must be clear that the words that follow are not meant to tell teachers how they should teach; the intention is to share some ideas. The public shouldn't tell teachers how to teach. But, rather, through public discussions, the public's views should be used to establish our guiding principles that drive teacher instruction.

Curriculum, in the case of the educators themselves, should not be left up to the preference of an individual or vary so wildly between states and institutions within the same state or from year to year. That is like leaving education up to luck. What to teach and how much emphasis to place on a subject should be decided based on the direction society needs its education system to go.

Boards of education are set up to guide direction of curricula, but, again turning to experience, the tendency would be to conclude that where they have not served us well is in not wanting many voices involved in their decisions. The result is the same as what we see occurring in our government in general; the system reacts too slowly when it isn't listening to the voice of the people. The result is too often a chosen direction that does not meet the people's needs.

Without knowing with certainty what teaching philosophy we believe in, we can't expect proper preparation of teachers, counselors, and administrators. If we keep drastically changing the target, the evaluation of teacher preparation becomes difficult. However, we still can consider the basic aspects of teacher preparation and quality assessment: pre-service teacher instruction, in-service teacher instruction, and teacher evaluation.

Pre-service instruction is the teachers' preparation through our colleges and universities prior to being hired as a teacher. Logically you would assume it includes defining their obligations as teachers, developing their understanding of how children learn best, honing their skills in recognizing learning difficulties, and expanding their subject matter knowledge base.

My overall impression of pre-service instruction has been that, like K–12 education, it has gaps, omissions, and inconsistencies. Once more turning to Seymour Sarason for his expertise on the subject, he provides several noteworthy points to consider in *The Case for Change: Rethinking the Preparation of Educators*. Sarason states that "preparatory programs inadequately prepare educators (teachers and administrators) for what life is like in classrooms, schools, and school systems," and that "preparatory programs unwittingly contribute to the manufacture of problems." And he proceeds to point out that "there has been little educational leadership to inform the general public about the whys and wherefores of prevention" (1993, 4).

Prevention of problems reasonably includes helping potential teachers understand their general obligations as classroom teachers. Pre-service instruction should emphasize principles like those set down by David P. Page in his 1847 book titled *Theory and Practice of Teaching*. An emphasis of his was that the teacher is "responsible for the morals, health, intellectual growth, and study habits of his pupils" (Good, 321).

Because of the reference to teaching morals, huffing and eye rolling is occurring. That reaction has been heard and seen before in meeting rooms. The reaction probably stems from the meaning of "morals" being greatly misunderstood and having a sexual connotation. "Morals" means "dealing with, or capable of making the distinction between, right and wrong in conduct" (*Webster's*, 1976). We know teaching morals is a responsibility of the home and community, but it must have been obvious back in 1847 that it needed to be emphasized in classrooms and therefore in teachers' training. Considering the world today versus back then, wouldn't acceptance of this responsibility be a step back in time moving toward correcting the incivility occurring in today's society?

Page also emphasized that the teacher "must teach pupils how to study intelligently, how to master the principles of science instead of preparing for a recitation or covering a book" (Good, 321). Science is the example in that statement but each subject has its own best ways to be taught, which the teaching profession refers to as "best practices." Teaching agreed-upon, researched-based best practices would work to further the goal of preventing problems.

Teachers and parents alike should understand the importance of the knowledge we now have concerning how children learn best. That knowledge should be guiding decisions on subject matter and technique. Scientific knowledge of brain development has helped identify what is developmentally appropriate to teach, meaning that we should recognize when a student is able to best comprehend a concept. Research has identified successful techniques. But the art of teaching is harder to understand and teach to teachers.

In veterinary medicine, some of the art of practice was in being able to read the body language of your patient. At times, it is a skill that can save a veterinarian's life. So stumbling on the children's book *Learning How to Learn* by L. Ron Hubbard (1992) felt like my life-saver. It was a moment in time that brought some welcomed clarity for our son and us.

As a parent, finding a book designed to help children, parents, and teachers in understanding the basics of learning was exhilarating and fun. It was a discovery worth sharing. Mentioning the name of the book to several administrators and teachers in various situations over many years, not a glimmer of interest was noted. Not one of "them" was curious enough to want to hear this perspective. That was not the case when mentioning it to other parents. This was back in 1995 and, having loaned the book out to parents until it didn't return, what is recalled here is from memory and the notes our son took.

In one section written to the adults, L. Ron Hubbard instructs the parent or teacher about the basics of recognizing the cues a child gives, what they might act like or their facial expressions, and how they feel when they are failing to learn. Most attentive mothers and fathers, like good teachers, probably already know this instinctively. That is part of the art of teaching; it's about reading children's signals. Hubbard then goes on to explain that, when they are having difficulties, it means they are experiencing a barrier to learning and only three barriers exist. They are: (1) lack of mass, meaning they are being presented with a concept they can't touch or see or conceptualize; (2) the missed step or too steep a learning gradient; and (3) the misunderstood word, the most commonly occurring barrier not only to learning but to communications in general for all of us.

The major portion of this book is the picture book itself designed for the children. L. Ron Hubbard teaches the child these same concepts in simple words with simple pictures. In each section, it has some mental exercises that include drawing and writing to illustrate and review the concepts he's teaching. The purpose of the book is to explain to children having trouble learning that when they experience confusion or difficulties learning they are still normal; they have just run into a barrier.

He teaches that a barrier is something that stops you. In the case of learning, it stops you from achieving understanding. When put into simplistic terms, these become concepts that parents and children, in addition to teachers, can understand, thus easily teaching all involved about learning how to learn. Concepts of barriers are taught to the teachers but probably in various ways and not in such simplistic terms as what is presented in this book.

In the educational field, they are trying to get at the same thing as "lack of mass" by saying children learn best when taught a concept "in context." However, after using this terminology of "taught in context" in a discussion with a college counselor, her confused look and the conversation that followed confirmed that it is not a universally understood concept or the terminology is not universal. The simplistic explanation that L. Ron Hubbard gives helps the child, parent, or teacher to understand that, if lack of mass is the difficulty, they need to find a picture, a thing, or a demonstration or relevant explanation to put a concept into a context that the child understands.

The missed step or too steep a teaching gradient clarifies that children need to learn things step-by-step or they may become confused. Hubbard compares it to following a recipe where, if you leave out one thing, if you miss an ingredient, it doesn't turn out right. His suggestion is to go back and find out where you went wrong, what step you missed. When you think about what this concept of a missed step means in an education system, if you are expecting middle school or high school teachers to go back and try to figure out the missed step for their students, the importance of teaching things right the first time should be clear to all.

For the misunderstood word, L. Ron Hubbard explains that you need to ask questions when confusion sets in and it may help clarify what word you have misunderstood. Or go back in your reading to where you last understood and reread until you come across the word that has tripped you up. He instructs to never go past a word you do not fully understand and gives the steps you should follow to "clear" the word. Clearing a word may include using a dictionary. He has also written a children's book on how to use a dictionary.

It was comforting and helpful to know of ways to help a child having difficulties learning and, remarkably, the troubles always seemed to fit into one of these three barriers in children with normal learning capacities. They weren't always something that could be fixed, like lack of phonics or a missed step in reading instruction. But others were doable, like finding or making a model of an atom when lack of mass was the barrier to understanding.

The greatest barrier, the misunderstood word, affects all our lives regularly. Look at the language barriers in medicine and education and the ongoing debate about English being our official language. What about the word "welfare" with a capital "W" and its use twice in the Constitution, or the word "preemptive"? Do we understand how those words were meant to be interpreted? Preempt can mean "to seize before anyone else can" (*Webster's*, 1976). Did we the people really understand its full meaning prior to entering Iraq? The misunderstood word is a huge concept.

If this book by L. Ron Hubbard, or something similar to it, could help us adults in understanding a child's learning difficulties, thus helping us more quickly come to a remedy for their confusion or failure, shouldn't we be using it in teacher education? In education they talk about remediation or remedial classes, but it appears to be a concept that has not been fully or consistently taught to teachers.

It is more difficult and time consuming to have to figure out years later what is at the root of any learning difficulty or how to fill gaps or correct mistakes. Recognition of problems is best done immediately. If you compare it to training an animal, it's always easier to make the correction of a teaching mistake immediately rather than let bad habits develop and have to totally retrain. Or compare it to any disease. It is always best to treat early in the course of the disease rather than wait while the disease causes further damage. Whenever possible, prevention is always preferred.

We should question how much attention is given in teacher preparation to recognition of learning difficulties, differences, and the development of an understanding of both verbal and nonverbal communication with relation to its importance in recognition and prevention of learning failures. In preparation to practice veterinary medicine, we considered recognition of nonverbal cues to be a basic element of successful clinical practice. My observations in the classrooms did not lead me to believe the same was true of the preparation of teachers. So, if that essential piece of educator preparation is missing, that fact probably explains why it appears that many teachers seem unaware of the nonverbal cues that they are sending out to children. This may be in something they do, or how they structure instruction.

Children are like small animals—no, they are animals. We all are, but children are just less domesticated than us adults. Children seem more in tune with their instincts than most adults and, therefore, more sensitive in general to the influences of others, especially those they look up to, as all young learners do their first teachers.

All first grade teachers need to be specially trained, considered experts, and respected as such. Multiple times over the years, regular first-year teachers have been placed in first grade classes. Some may have done fine, but were steps missed? Would they do things differently, better, the next time around? If a child only does first grade once, can we risk potentially creating a problem and expecting the next teacher to figure out what went wrong? We must do things right the first time. First grade is critical. First grade must be a successful experience for all children. The only way to ensure that is with proper instruction and individual attention to the learning needs of the child. That has to be accomplished with exceptional, specially trained teachers in smaller classes.

Teachers have been taught, and we have accepted as fact, that children must learn to read by third grade. Yet observations show us that kids know by second grade if they are behind and they begin to compensate. Later on, that compensation is called cheating. We may have until third grade to turn children into independent readers. That isn't the same thing as accepting that letting them leave first grade without the reading skills they need is all right. Are we misunderstanding? We need to question the conventional wisdom that we have until third grade to teach them to read. First grade teachers must be taught to do things right the first time.

Other specialized teacher instruction is important, too. Not enough educators in the middle schools have specialized in middle school instruction. This partially explains the particular failures of our middle and high school curricula and instruction.

The Trends in International Math and Science Study (TIMSS) report concluded that the United States was doing a competitive job in the early grades with math and science instruction but our students then would start to lose ground by eighth grade (Valverde, Schmidt, 1997–1998). Combining that conclusion with the fact that we have large dropout rates in many of our schools should lead us to suspect something is amiss in the middle and high schools around the country.

This phenomenon is not the fault of teachers; they have not been given the information they need. Teaching the importance of the functions and purpose of middle schools and high schools appears to have been swept out with the tide of standards and testing. Our middle schools or junior high schools were supposed to function as the bridge between the elementary school and high school. The purpose of the middle school was to help the student stay on the bridge to avoid falling into the turbulent waters created by the adolescent period. That work requires the collaborative effort of family, church, and community to be successful. And the need for professional, well-trained counselors is an essential and apparently neglected piece of the story.

Consistency is a must at this stage. Specialized instruction of teachers, counselors, administrators, and parents about the unique developmental changes of the adolescent period would go a long way toward fixing and preventing the special problems associated with adolescence. The same story holds true for the high schools.

The high schools' function is to finish the preparation of students to transition into the "real world." This may mean preparing them for college or a vocation. This dual function of the high school is why prior student assessment and proper guidance is important in making the high school function as intended.

The extreme importance of an effective counseling program can't be stressed enough. Neither can the importance of continuing and intensifying the involvement of the community because, at one point in time, the purpose of a high school was considered to be to act as the center of a community and serve as a center of activity.

These ideals and ideas are not new and have been explored in depth, along with other relevant issues, in the previously referenced *Cooperative Study of Secondary School Standards.* This study's findings have not been taught to all secondary school teachers, administrators, and counselors or drawn any widespread public attention. Instead, we are blindly looking for the answers to the woes of high schools when our government has already studied the subject intently. The current powers that be may not even know of the existence of this information, for war had disrupted the progress of this project as it had similarly with the American Lyceum and other worthwhile projects. The purpose of the study was to improve functioning of secondary schools (the middle or junior high and high schools) through an "active self-improvement process." The importance of the counselor's role in secondary schools was particularly emphasized as was the importance of community.

When talking about high schools, one particular group of schools in Providence, Rhode Island—referred to as the Met—deserves mention in that they have shown improved graduation rates and have earned high marks from parents. On a measure for parental involvement that was designed to assess how involved parents feel in the school and how comfortable they are with teachers and school environment, the 2006 Rhode Island State Report Card statistics show 80 percent of parents had positive responses compared with 42 percent for the state.

Their instructional plans are based on learning through internships. The first of these schools was the subject of a 2002 book by Eliot Levine where he explained that "learning happens best when tailored to each student's needs," thus the title *One Kid at a Time: Big Lessons from a Small School.* Many aspects of these Met schools deserve consideration, including the ideas of interest-based learning, a balance of needs and interests, learning through doing, small student-to-"advisor" ratio, community involvement through mentors and internships, a set of expectations that includes personal qualities, and a view that "parents are essential partners whose input shapes the student's learning activities" (2002, 97).

The aspects of the schools that make them successful were not things that were put in place through a program. Rather, it appears to have begun with a person with a vision. That vision was then more clearly focused, and continues to be focused, based on the exchange of ideas between administration, educators, students, parents, and community members. Through this ongoing process, the staff has developed a shared vision and has attempted—it appears, successfully—to build a community of learners that includes all but is centered around the value in each student. It sounds like they model what it means to have respect for each other's opinions and what can result when high expectations for learning are set, for real, and in real-life settings. How many of these basic philosophies about how children learn and the processes for school improvement are taught in our teacher, counselor, and administrator preparation classes?

In talking about teacher preparation, we have jumped from first grade to high school. But the idea is to clear up the misunderstanding that what you see happening in ineffective classrooms is always the fault of the teacher. The experimentation in teaching techniques that were expounded upon earlier as being less than successful were not a reflection on the teacher. It wasn't a bad teacher; it was inadequate teacher instruction.

Our colleges and universities need to establish improved teacher training programs with the aim of preventing the large inconsistencies that are currently occurring. Our children's education system deserves an effort greater than that of other professions to make pre-service curricula consistent, relevant to our children's needs, and geared toward preventing problems as much as possible. This effort to improve teacher training is going to take collaboration of higher education with teachers associations and organizations, the business world, and the public. Common ground must be established to proceed effectively.

Once pre-service preparation becomes more dependable, then in-service education can be used more efficiently. "In-service" is terminology that is interchangeable with staff development or professional development and is called continuing education in most professions.

Professional development of existing teachers must include assessing their deficits in understanding and filling those gaps. Those words make the job sound easy. But the time and money it is going to require, particularly in "failed" districts, make the effectiveness and efficiency of staff development extremely important. It should not be approached in just any manner. It must be well-planned, focused, and doable with all involved parties in agreement on the direction. Now it sounds complicated.

Professional development in science education, if you recall, was not so long ago my focus of research for grant writing purposes. Like with most fields of study in education, many experts and much information abound. It is worth sharing again that what appeared in the research to be the best approach is based on taking individuals from whatever level of understanding or proficiency they are at and bringing all to a higher level.

Teacher professional development should always be done with the concerns of the teacher in mind and with adequate time for adaptation to the philosophies and ideas presented prior to any changes in the classroom. The idea is not to tell them how to teach but to help them teach in their own way, only better.

Unfortunately, many teachers now think of professional development as time spent in learning about a new program that is changed with a change of administration or on the whim of a new fad. Our efforts need to change to focusing our professional development of teachers, counselors, and administrators on:

> ➢ the educational principles we value;

> ➢ the elements of how children learn best specific to their population of learners;

> ➢ how to identify and remedy problems they are seeing in their classrooms;

> ➢ updates on what resources are available within a community to help with remedies; and

> ➢ the content knowledge of the subject or subjects they teach.

Many parts of the country and even areas within this state seem to have settled the question of what to teach and how to best go about it. But until we find consistency in our beliefs and desires about the direction of education and on teacher pre-service and in-service preparation, the discussion of evaluation of teachers is perhaps a moot point.

In this discussion, teacher evaluations are not in reference to the routine evaluations by principals but rather what the teaching profession might consider ways to handle the problem of individuals within their profession who do not meet the standards of the profession.

In veterinary medicine, competency is based on the locally accepted standard of practice. When a client feels a violation of the standard of practice has occurred, a complaint is lodged and an investigation by a board of peers takes place. If the complaint is found to be valid, punishment ensues. The punishment could include continuing education in the area of practice where the violation occurred, but it can also mean removal from practice. That is my understanding of the process. Thankfully, that is not taken from personal experience.

The point is, teaching is a profession and like other professions it is the professionals themselves that should take the responsibility for evaluating themselves. It is an impossible task without defining the expectations of the profession. It is currently a fact that we can't define and measure what good teaching is to the satisfaction of our society. The merit pay movement currently being debated in this state is being based largely on our achievement tests. Yet our standards have been criticized severely on a national level. This state is not alone. Do we really want to evaluate teachers based on inadequate standards and tests whose accuracy and relevance has also been questioned? And this leads to improvement how? Consider that even excellent teachers, by whatever standard you make that judgment, can have their efforts thwarted if they don't have the resources to do their jobs.

The Materials to Do It

> The time has therefore come when a plan of universal education ought to be adopted in the United States.
>
> George Washington

Failure to provide the materials for all our students to succeed in school is a long-standing problem. We as a nation should be ashamed of the fact that we have not addressed it. We pontificate about our children being our greatest resource. We talk about investing in our future, our children. We say we value education. We state that we understand its importance to the future of our democracy. But we don't put our money where our mouths are.

Materials always cost money. And, to spend money wisely, you have to have a plan that helps you identify the materials essential to reaching your goal. Even without a plan, we know that material support for education consists of everything from the buildings themselves to books, paper and pencils, science and technology equipment, educators' pay, and, of course, the currently overshadowing cost of testing. This is the place for the business world to help education. It isn't by supplying the materials to which I refer where we need their help; it is help needed conducting a serious review and evaluation of the spending throughout the educational bureaucracy and the government in general.

The common people of the United States have cut back their spending. It's time for our government to cut back so we can afford to fund education properly. Our government systems need to develop the efficiency and effectiveness that are currently only buzzwords. These words are wrongly being applied to the classroom when, instead, they should be applied to the wasteful governing structure that we have created.

The building of school buildings is a perfect example. Over the many years of attending school board meetings, the board has spent countless hours in discussion over a building's features and aesthetic appeal. They never spent that kind of time in public debating whether it is time to reduce our first grade class sizes to fifteen students to ensure that we begin the job of educating by doing it right from the start. They never spent that much time on discussing whether we have a sufficient number of books in our secondary schools to teach proper study habits.

Instead, the school architects happily present yet another new design for our board to proudly attach their names. Over the years, as a watchful taxpayer, it has been unclear at times whether the essential elements of a healthy, efficient building were foremost. In the animal industry, we have used science to determine the required elements of efficient buildings and have disseminated that knowledge through the Cooperative Extension Services for producers to use. But consider, all over the country, local boards continue to independently spend taxpayer dollars on architecture and design fees unknowingly spending dollars that could better be spent elsewhere. A duty of the U.S. Department of Education as outlined in the Smith-Towner Bill was to "conduct studies and investigations in the field of education and to report thereon" (1920, 577). All these meetings, all the individual school building plans, and the national report on the essential elements of healthy school buildings has not been discussed. Does it exist? Has no one considered our local tax dollars important enough to assist us in using them wisely?

This subject of materials is all about money. Unfortunately, that is a fact we cannot get around, nor can we get around the fact that currently money spent for education and the politics tied to that money cannot soon be separated. In observing the politics of my time develop, it has appeared that our government would cut education dollars whenever financial panic arose. That panic has more often been caused by our overspending on wars.

When reading about the history of education through H. G. Good, one should be taken aback to hear him make the same observation of the past and his time. His book was published the year I was born. His conclusion was that this society does not sufficiently support its schools. And he offered a cure. It is "to be found in fuller information. To doubt this is to doubt that the public is genuinely favorable to good education" (1956, 17–18).

The Plus Marks, Communicate and Cooperate

It takes a great man to be a good listener.

Calvin Coolidge

Communications and cooperation—they aren't small words. They are huge words that, when their impact on the educational formula is considered, function as the stir stick in the beaker; they become essential to the mixing of the elements of success. And, in thinking about these words, the ability to listen to one another is an element common to both.

Do governing boards, politicians, and administrators find themselves unable to listen? Did they not learn that skill in school or at home? Or have they just chosen not to listen? The unwillingness or inability to listen appears to be a major factor contributing to not only our problems in education but other social problems as well.

Resultant civil unrest is beginning to surface in a variety of public arenas from pollution of local land and water, to control of our media by monopolies; the stories all sound the same. You, the public, go to public meetings where the voiced consensus is the same as your own. But you later hear that the final decision is not what you heard voiced at the public meeting. This type of blatant disregard for public opinion demonstrates a lack of respect for the democratic process. We can forgive these people for not recognizing that they are giving into the cult of professionalism and putting themselves or their group's interests ahead of the public's. But we must go on to attempt to teach them better about what it really means to work for the public.

We should and we can teach others how to listen. And we can teach about the cult of professionalism and the political principle and its effect on our ability to listen to one another. We all belong to a cult of professionalism. You don't have to be labeled a professional to join. Parents do it: we know best. Philanthropists, corporations, and politicians do it: they know best. Barriers to listening must be understood for us to overcome them. Both communications and cooperation are improved from learning about and coming to an understanding of why we all build barriers around ourselves. Ultimately this means you come to recognize why you don't want to listen and recognize that you must listen in order to respect and consider the other person's opinion.

In *Fahrenheit 451*, a novel by Ray Bradbury about book burning, his character Faber says, "I saw the way things were going, a long time back. I said nothing. . . . Nobody listens any more" (1953, 82). You can't make people listen but each of us can recognize that we should and begin to practice listening regularly. Of course, that alone does not increase our chances of communicating effectively. As Mr. Bradbury goes on to point out, other things need to occur for information to make a difference in people's lives. Through his character Montag, the wise old man, Bradbury makes clear the importance of "1) the quality of the information, 2) the leisure to digest it, and 3) the right to carry out actions based on what we learn from the interaction of the first two" (84). And if people are not using terminology you are familiar with, the quality of the information is lost right away.

Educators and scientists are well known for not being trained to communicate well to the general public. They tend to use words or acronyms that are common to their own areas of expertise but unknown to ordinary people. This can leave the general public feeling stupid and, certainly, that won't lead to understanding. In veterinary medicine, we were trained, and hopefully we all learned from experience, that we need to communicate in terms that the person we are addressing can understand. Educators are aware of this same concept but consistency in practice of good communications skills is still lacking.

So the necessity to develop communications, with the intention of creating an informed public in order to build cooperation, must be addressed by communities and our learning institutions alike. A community education coordinator could help in bridging the gaps by working toward clarifying language usage and improving communications. But the ultimate solution to our lack of cooperation within our government, with regard to education, can only be found when an open discussion of their role in education is defined and clarified by the people.

The Equal Sign

Equality, in the American sense of the word, is not an end but a beginning. It means that, so far as the state can do it, all children shall start in the race of life on an even line. The chief agency for this purpose is the public school system.

Edwin E. Slosson

In the education equation presented, what would the equal sign represent? What is the equalizer? Those are the questions I asked myself in order to write this section.

The first answer was easy. On a day-to-day basis, that would be the principal of the school. The principal needs to know the students, know the teachers, know what materials are needed, and have a clear vision of the goals of each grade level or subject, in addition to understanding the teaching process and receiving input from teachers, students, and parents. The principal that knows and can do all of that is the one person in a position to evaluate students' progress toward being educated. The principal is the most important administrator in the hierarchy of school administration. Our success in schools depends on them, thus making their training and continued training of extreme importance. For, in addition to what has been listed, they must also know the policies and laws governing their school.

Laws would be my second answer to what should act as an equalizer. This is a harder answer to discuss because it isn't holding true in our republic today. We are supposed to be a land of law-abiding citizens but multiple examples exist of laws we choose to ignore.

Some laws are unfair and other laws we know nothing about. The Smith-Towner Bill that established the U.S. Department of Education and the position of secretary of education is a law unknown to me until recently. As a citizen wanting to clarify the purpose of the U.S. Department of Education and the function of the secretary, it seemed essential to have the information that this bill contained. As told to me by my local librarian and confirmed by the U.S. Department of Education, the knowledge contained in that law is knowledge that the ordinary citizen needs to pay to obtain.

It turns out that, in addition to setting appropriations of money, the Smith-Towner Bill set the duty of the Department of Education to research and report on six areas of education. Those areas are: "1) illiteracy, 2) immigrant education, 3) public-school education, and especially rural education, 4) physical education, including health education, recreation and sanitation, 5) preparation and supply of competent teachers for the public schools, and 6) in such other fields as, in the judgment of the Secretary of Education, may require attention and study" (1920, 577). This bill goes on to point out that it came into existence to encourage the following: removal of illiteracy, Americanization, physical education, and improvement of educational opportunities through improved teacher preparation and in-service, increased teacher salaries, and extension of public libraries and other opportunities. In order to participate in the funding, they had set as requirements that a school would be in session at least twenty-four weeks, that all children ages seven to fourteen had to attend, and that the English language would be the basic language of instruction.

In one newspaper debate of that time, the removal of illiteracy appeared to be the biggest selling point for establishment of the U.S. Department of Education. Reading that article led to inquiring about the current illiteracy rate in the United States. The men and women answering the phones at the U.S. Department of Education do an excellent job of answering questions about No Child Left Behind. They have been well trained on that subject. Answering this question was different. The result was a long wait on hold, a phone number to call, and an apology for not having the answer. It certainly wasn't her fault. It just demonstrated the shift of our emphasis that has taken place over time. We are obviously out of touch with our roots, our beginnings, our purpose, and our own laws.

The Smith-Towner Bill was a nine-page bill written in 1920. The debate at the time in favor of it was that it was seen as the only way to improve the illiteracy rate. The argument against it was that it would expose the states to the potentially corrupt influences of national politics. We might consider opening that debate anew. And now may be the time.

Johnson's 1965 Elementary and Secondary Education Act was an attempt by the federal government to make right the wrong that is being done to our poor and neglected children. And, at that time, local districts appeared to be using the funds appropriately, as judged by the secretary of health, education, and welfare, Wilbur J. Cohen. His opinion was that the money was going to "activities most directly serving the student's needs: improving the quality of instruction and offering such services as medical care, guidance and counseling, and food" (Congressional Quarterly, 1969, 711).

That was then. Here we are now with our nine-hundred-plus-page No Child Left Behind bill that even I don't care to read, so I'll never understand how it can act as an equalizer, if that is its intention. Possibly it is time for the Federalist Papers to be required reading for lawmakers. If this reading doesn't put them to sleep, they might pick up on Alexander Hamilton's words in *The Federalist*, no. 25, where he said, "Wise politicians will be cautious about fettering the government with restrictions, that cannot be observed" (December 21, 1787).

How can the NCLB law serve the people as a guide and how can the people have any part in enforcement and accountability of laws we don't understand? It appears to be time to question the wisdom of our politicians. Laws are not serving as the equalizer that they should be; neither is money.

Unfortunately, money is the third answer as to what could be an equalizer. Money has been discussed in talking about providing the materials necessary for educational opportunity. It is a tough thing for some ordinary Americans to have to admit its power as an equalizer in education. Our funding formulas and the hodgepodge granting systems we have devised have led to greater inequalities and lost dollars in administering programs and granting grants.

What H. G. Good had pointed out, in reference to philanthropic monies, can be applied to the federal granting system: grants have created a situation where we are "offering a full meal to a fortunate few but only crumbs to the many" (1956, 141). This is another place where the great business minds of our country could really help by devising a way to gradually change funding procedures without disturbing the functioning of our schools in the process.

With insight and vision, together, we could provide funding aimed at ensuring equal educational opportunity. My faith in the innovative ways of Americans is intact. We can provide equal educational opportunities if we set our minds and hearts on that goal.

Equal Educational Opportunity

The democracy which proclaims equality of opportunity as its ideal requires an education in which learning and social application, ideas and practice, work and recognition of the meaning of what is done, are united from the beginning and for all.

John Dewey

What does equal educational opportunity mean? Equal education does not mean the same education for all. Perhaps we should be thinking about it as relevant education—not the same education—for all. Perhaps we should be considering equal opportunity to a relevant education as our goal. We the people need to answer this question, for it is the over-riding question whose answer should guide all our plans. To take aim, we must identify the target. The target has become blurred by our insistence on standards and testing. In setting test scores as our goal, we have gone totally against the findings of the *Evaluation of Secondary Schools*.

Their objection to testing as a sole method of accreditation or for similar widespread comparison was that testing tends to make "instruction point definitely to success in examinations," cultivates "a uniformity that is deadening to instruction," can "thwart the initiative of instructors," and can "destroy the flexibility and individuality of an institution" (1939, 163). In addition to it bringing about a rigid curriculum, they concluded this type of testing had little validity for identifying superior and inferior schools and felt a better method was available.

This study also clearly stated in their chapter on guiding principles what they determined to be the desired results of the learning process. They felt it should include factual information or knowledge, meaning and understanding, an ability to combine knowledge and understanding with skill, desirable attitudes, worthy ideals, purposes, appreciations, interests, and resultant intelligent participation in general life activities. Are these still our guiding principles?

Look closely and you may find we all want the same things and they are stated for us in the guiding principles of the *Cooperative Study of Secondary School Standards*. If you don't agree, let's at least agree that the time has come for us to make known our desired direction for education—not standards but guiding principles. It's our duty given the fact that education professionals seem incapable of changing their system. It appears that a catalyst has become a crucial ingredient to making this reaction produce.

The Catalyst: The Public

All measures designed to promote education must depend for their success, in this country, on the hearty cooperation of public opinion. It is only by enlightening and concentrating that opinion that powerful effects can be produced.

Horace Mann

I believe that the majority of people here in the United States do care about education or would care if they understood the situation and understood that hope for the system does exist. Understanding must start with knowing the facts. We need to analyze, discuss, and face the facts. We must also question the facts to get to the truth.

Without the truth, the public can't provide the check and balance they should to see through the idea of creating an effectively functioning educational system that provides equal educational opportunity. It deserves repeating: it is our duty as citizens to get all pertinent facts and pursue the needed improvements. Change will only come about through people, both in and outside the system, who have the desire in their hearts to do what is right. The political system must work with the people to get this done. We must develop that common understanding and common vision to guide us toward the goal of equal opportunity that thus far has eluded us. The process has been started before.

In 1955 President Eisenhower called the White House conference on education. According to an account of it by H. G. Good, "Connecticut reported her problems were the universal ones; the shortage of teachers, buildings, and finances and the lack of effective ways and means to gain and hold a lively and well-informed public interest in the schools. The conference members concluded that they should deal with: (1) the need for school construction, (2) the educational aims/ what the schools should accomplish, (3) economic and efficient organization, (4) recruitment and retention of good teachers, (5) financing of schools, and (6) maintenance of public interest in schools" (1956, 558). It was felt at the time that stimulation of public interest in schools had been an achievement of the conference, and it was reported that the participants walked away feeling that "if local and state conferences were continued as planned in some areas, the White House Conference will have been a success" (558).

In the Western Historical Manuscript Collection through the University of Missouri–St. Louis, a trace of that conference can be found in a report of the St. Louis–St. Louis County White House Conference on Education that boasts to have "established effective communication among lay citizens, educators, and legislators; and its recommendations have served as guides to developing policy, public understanding, and legislative support." In addition, they claim to have brought in "experts to speak on vital issues in education."

The hope is that by now these ideas are sounding familiar. The hope is that it is starting to become clear that we have talked and analyzed the subject of education to death throughout the history of the United States. Now the time is upon us to pause and reflect long and hard about the road that led us to this point and the change in direction that we wish to take. Our children need us to choose wisely this time.

We need to understand where we have failed in the past for we have been warned by our forefathers that "if we are not cautious to avoid a repetition of the error, in our future attempts to rectify and ameliorate our system, we may travel from one chimerical project to another; we may try change after change; but we shall never be likely to make any material change for the better" (*The Federalist*, no. 26, Alexander Hamilton, December 22, 1787).

We have failed to maintain lasting educational reform in the past and will again unless we understand our errors. Reform is not a bad word. It is not a word that should be associated with a political party. Reform means "to make better by removing faults and defects or to make better by putting a stop to abuses or malpractices or by introducing better procedures" (*Webster's*, 1976). But reform has failed.

Thanks to my son's interest and enthusiasm for history, which was a gift from an excellent teacher, I stumbled upon the keys to the understanding of the failure of reforms within the pages of *The Age of Reform* by Richard Hofstadter. He discusses Josiah Strong's theory that "if public opinion is educated concerning a given reform—political, social, industrial, or moral—and if the popular conscience is sufficiently awake to enforce an enlightened public opinion, the reform is accomplished straightaway" (1955, 202). Hofstadter went on to point out through the writings of William Allen White that "the only permanent cure was in changing the system" (259). The reformers of the Progressive period had failed to do that. Hofstadter also stated, "History cannot quite repeat itself, if only because the participants in the second round of any experience are aware of the outcome of the first" (313). Unfortunately, he was wrong when that theory is applied to educational history. He seemed to have not envisioned a world in which the people didn't read each other's work or works from the past. He did, however, see the wrong assumption in Strong's belief that reform could work.

Richard Hofstadter's conclusion was that reform required laws and enforcement of laws required political leadership with moral quality. He wrote, with what can be perceived as a mocking tone, that others believed that reforms could be upheld despite the "relaxed moral vigilance" of citizens, provided the people "choose men of the highest moral qualities" for political leaders. He points out that "it was assumed that such moral qualities were indestructible and that decent men, once found and installed in office, would remain decent. When they had regained control of affairs, moral rigor would not flag again" (202).

We all would like to elect the person to solve our problems for us. We would like to elect the person that has vision, principles in line with our own, and integrity. That we must participate fully in the political process ourselves seems to be something we don't care to do. Or we don't understand how we can do it with everything else that is demanding of our time and efforts. Some may think we have no way out of this political mess that we have created, which is blocking our progress in education and now on multiple fronts with various crises. Others just know it is essential that we do find our way.

J. M. Rice was one person that clearly saw the need to tackle the issue of politics in education. Dr. Rice was particularly impressed with German education and based his conclusions on his observations there, as compared to the United States classrooms that he observed. In 1893, he wrote *The Public School System of the United States*. He suggested three things that were necessary to improve the city schools: (1) drive out the politicians, (2) train and keep training teachers so curriculum could be indefinitely broadened without detriment to the Three Rs, and (3) provide competent supervision (Good, 398).

Other more recent authors also offer solutions to our political dilemma. Kevin Phillips's book titled *Arrogant Capital* offers some interesting insight into how we might begin to "reclaim the people's role in governing our country." In the last chapter of that book, he offers proposals that include the idea of "decentralizing or dispersing power away from Washington" (1994, 186). That particular proposal is well suited to address the changes needed in education. Education is not benefiting from the influence of lobbyists. Political influence is not an essential ingredient of quality education—the influence of the people is.

The negative influences of politics on education have been noted previously, with NCLB being our most current and striking example. Unfortunately, breaking the political stronghold on education is both necessary and a thought that most people don't really want to consider. Change is difficult. It scares us because once it begins you can't know with certainty where it might lead. Fear can keep us from acting.

But when you believe in acting thoughtfully and with common sense, with exchange of ideas and consensus as your guides, change becomes desirable. No harm needs to come to the American children that we have promised to provide with equal educational opportunity. I have tried to live my adult life and practice in my profession by following the first law of medicine—above all else, do no harm. We can do the same for all the children of the United States.

The radical changes inflicted upon us by our government through the dictates of No Child Left Behind harmed a generation of children by wasting their instructional time and not giving them equal access to the promised benefits. Where were the leaders who are charged with looking out for the greater good of the people? Where were the people?

When we were leading the world educationally, we didn't need international benchmarks or standards set for us; we, the American people, knew what we needed to do to get ahead. We know enough now to proceed responsibly in addressing the needs of underperforming schools and in improving teacher and principal quality for all.

The blame for the "educationally deprived children" not being provided educational opportunity officially lies with state and local officials. The federal government has attempted to make good on the promise of equality but does not provide adequate funding and does not understand enough about the education system to fix it. The people do; we have the answers.

The time is always right to do what is right.

Martin Luther King Jr.

CHAPTER SEVEN
WHAT'S NEXT?

Perhaps the sentiments contained in the following pages, are not yet sufficiently fashionable to procure them general favor; a long habit of not thinking a thing wrong, gives it a superficial appearance of being right, and raises at first a formidable outcry in defense of custom. But the tumult soon subsides. Time makes more converts than reason.

Thomas Paine

Intuitively, the common people know it is time to do what is right. The instincts of everyday people have them feeling the urgency of their needs, telling them that time is running out, that we aren't going to get many more chances to get things right, that change must occur soon. It is time for reason and common sense to lead.

The ordinary Americans are usually the ones to roll up their sleeves and get a job done. But the focus and direction that transformation should take in education, or in our republic as a whole, is still unclear for many. That is because by failing to inform the public of the knowledge we have gained through research in the education field and about the change process, we have failed to use that knowledge to its fullest benefit. We appear to not know how to take the steps to put that change process in motion.

For me, it truly is the time to do what is right. It is right to speak out honestly and strongly about the educational needs of our children and our society as a whole. It is time to put aside our differences on divisive cultural issues and work together to solve the problems that are looming over us, threatening to take us under. Have our actions demonstrated the ideal that we are united as a people?

Hurricane Katrina supposedly pointed out not only bureaucratic failings but also the state of poverty and ignorance within an area of our United States. It pointed to a failed public education system that many outraged Americans vowed to get behind and fix. Have we? Some are trying and some reform is occurring, but, according to the Center for Education Reform, Louisiana ranked forty-seventh in the United States in achievement scores, which wouldn't be bad if we were a country like Finland, where the disparity between the highest and lowest student scores is not that great. But that is not the case in the United States. According to that same report, Louisiana is only graduating 63 percent of its students, and it isn't at the bottom of that list! We won't leave Iraq without victory but we leave school after school behind. Did we forget about these kids once they were no longer in the news? Do we the people know and understand what we are letting go?

It is time we face the fact that we do not have a large enough pool of well-educated American citizens to fill all the essential jobs for a successful, prosperous, democratic society: scientists, health care professionals, educators, and political leaders. Many industries and institutions have turned to importing better-educated workers or outsourcing work. That works for corporate America but not for Congress.

Unless we are ready to give up our sovereignty as a nation to the idea of being only a part of a global union, we need educated American political leaders to fill all our congressional seats. We need wise men and women that know enough about science and economics, in addition to the Constitution of the United States, to do the job that they are supposed to do. Congress does not even seem to understand that "the fabric of American Empire ought to rest on the solid basis of The Consent of the People. The streams of national power ought to flow immediately from that pure original fountain of all legitimate authority" (*The Federalist*, no. 22, Alexander Hamilton, December 14, 1787).

We, as a united nation, have failed to answer a question basic to both educational improvement and the ideals of a democracy or a republic itself: Whose job is it to keep the public informed? We talk about the Founding Fathers and our Constitution's significance to us, but we ignore the words of the first president of the United States as he was leaving office. We have failed to see his true significance. George Washington was the first to experience the implementation of our great plan, our great experiment, to establish a republic different from the failings of other great republics. And, in his reflections on that experience, found in his Farewell Address to Congress, a document of over six thousand words, he spoke of promoting "institutions for the general diffusion of knowledge."

We are accustomed to the laundry list of wants expressed by our modern-day presidents in their State of the Union addresses. The context in which George Washington spoke about "diffusion of knowledge" was surprising. In this address, he reviewed beliefs and principles on which the Constitution was written and which a republic needs to follow to survive. The "institutions for the general diffusion of knowledge" was the only item that he promoted. The lack of an institution charged with diffusing knowledge was what our first president saw as a deficit within this experiment to build a lasting republic based on our "free Constitution."

It was over two hundred years ago that he gave that speech. Today, we have yet to sufficiently promote that concept. Education's time to be seen as a national priority has come. Perception is said to be through the lens of experience. Through George Washington's experiences he could see what was missing in the experiment but could not see how to add the necessary ingredient. We now have had two hundred additional years of experience; do we see it yet?

Many great men that valued our union, and valued education's role in it, did not see through the implementation of a plan to provide universal education. The need for that provision was acknowledged by many; it is not a radical idea. It is not a call for sweeping reform but instead a call for effective changes in the governing structure of education.

The classroom itself should be the last place for the change to occur. Classrooms should be where we see our goals realized. Much work needs to be done outside the classroom first. We must be as certain as we can that no harm is done; no learning time is wasted. But, let me be very clear, it is a complete change from a dysfunctional bureaucracy to a functioning system that is needed to provide equality in educational opportunity. I hope you listen openly to my reasoning.

The hope is that you see education as key to economic development, as essential to the practice of preventative medicine, as paramount to quick change in our global climate disaster, and as the backbone of democracy. The hope is that these are concepts every one of you thoughtfully considers.

We may not have the time left to only improve one school full of children at a time. We don't know from what geographical location or layer of society our best and brightest will sprout forth. We can't afford to let any of them wilt. We must do our best to ensure all our schools equally offer opportunity.

Each time a new school is set up in a manner different from our current traditional public schools, it attracts and selects the best teachers it can find. They continue to leave the "old" schools behind, which limits the opportunity for some students to have exposure to the best. Each time a new school is set up, it attracts parents who care about education, effectively removing their influence from the old schools. Some children are helped while others may be hurt. We call this "choice" and the process is called "reform." We must consider the unintentional results of this type of reform.

When parents feel they are forced to choose a school other than their local neighborhood school, it adds further to the break-up and deterioration of some neighborhoods. It may disconnect the children and their families from other families in their immediate surroundings. And we tend to think of schools as institutions and assume they have institutional memory of the important desires and traditions of their people. The reality is that, with the mobility of staff, institutional memory is lost. That aspect of stability becomes dependent on families.

We must also consider that an unintentional result of local reforms is that it pacifies many of us concerned about our nation's educational standing in the world and those of us concerned about all of our children's education. If you are only looking out for your own child, reform may work. But it never "fixes" the education system. It only makes change one school at a time.

If you are looking out for the general welfare of the common people in the quest for that more perfect union, revolutionary change is our only hope. Reform and choice satisfies some. It satisfies the right people. It satisfies enough of us to keep us from revolting.

Where to Begin?

Recently I found a note to myself in the back of a notepad. It said, "What have we learned? If something isn't 'clicking,' don't move on; go back."

In every experiment, failed or successful, a lesson is to be learned. In the analysis of a problem, go back and review the arguments. Let's go back and see if we can begin anew, with understanding.

In this case, go back to the model of action shown in chapter 3; where's the science? It illustrates that the base for change, the support for the pyramid, should be research and best practices followed by the development of a shared vision.

Throughout this book were scattered small bits of research and mention of a few of the researchers who have gone into developing a vision of what needs to happen next. That is a minute fraction of the research that exists. No one can know it all. We don't need to if we work together. Collectively, we know so much, yet we seem paralyzed when it comes to making real change in the education system. Knowledge, no matter how good and relevant, does us no good if we can't or won't put it to work for us. We have knowledge but no responsible comprehensive plan of action. Muriel Lester talked about "the sin of being negative instead of positive . . . we theorized and argued, but we did not act . . . we had no clear aim" (1940, 15).

Go back again, this time to the formula for success in chapter 6 and look at the elements and components that were discussed as being essential to success. Think about the various subjects taught in schools. And, most important, use whatever knowledge, observations, and experiences you have had with children to focus your thoughts on how children develop and how they learn. Decide for yourself what your priorities would be if it was you having the final say in deciding a significant change to our education system. Or just pick an area of interest and start small and locally. What one thing would you choose to focus your aim on?

The choice of where and how to get involved is yours to make. Start big or small, local or nationally, at the top or bottom, it doesn't matter; it all makes a difference. But as a nation, for the system of education to develop to its fullest potential, we must begin by asking the center of our existing education system, our colleges and universities, to provide us guidance. They have been the constant strength and pride of our American education system. They have the researchers. They have the experts. And they are producing our next generation of teachers.

Rhona Weinstein likened the sequence of schooling to a pipeline, indicating that universities are "the last station in the pipeline." Liking the analogy but seeing through a different lens, consider the perspective that they are the first station; they control the spigot. Higher education personnel must become more significant in taking the lead. Seymour Sarason wrote, "If and when educational theorists, researchers, and policy experts in our universities participate in the discussion, we have reason to be somewhat hopeful" (1993, 269–270).

This is the time for having high hopes. But, so far nationally, higher education personnel have not been successful at using the change process to spread their knowledge in order to develop a broad base of support, at using that support to develop a vision, or in putting a true vision in motion. They need help. The colleges and universities need help from those below them, for what it appears these highly intellectual individuals seem to lack is the ability to reach the common people with their research. Maybe they don't realize that the common people are the ones needed to drive the needed changes. The researchers in education know research continues, results vary, one study contradicts another, but they need help coming to the realization that we must forge on using common sense in deciding what is right for our children and what practices will help us move toward providing true equity in learning opportunities for the children in our respective communities.

These debates on research can't be kept within institutional walls. We have children in classrooms depending on us to make wise, informed decisions. It's time to meet that challenge. Give what knowledge you have to the people, so they can make use of it in deciding what we Americans value in education. We need the knowledge to evaluate what is going on in our schools and to thoughtfully question our own decisions; Is it for the common good, or will it do harm? Or, as Alexander Hamilton might logically ask, is it necessary and proper?

Many ideals and ideas have been presented for your consideration. To illustrate how we might put these concepts into a plan that puts our knowledge into action, let's go through a few easy examples.

How It Works

To begin, let's imagine that we are in a community that has an education coordinator in place. The coordinator has gathered and recorded statistics, surveyed the stakeholders, assessed the available relevant resources, and developed a plan of attack for communications. The topics of interest and concern to the community have centered around three major themes: kids ready to learn, teachers ready to teach, and support of learning materials.

When discussing the subject of having kids ready to learn, a recurrent theme voiced by a variety of community members and teachers was the need for respect both in the schools and in the community in general. Suggestions were gathered and exploration produced a local expert willing to come, present research on the topic, and lead a discussion. The expert was politely given instruction on communicating in simple terms and asked to keep in-depth statistics to a minimum.

The expert proceeded to do an excellent job of reminding us that respect is essential to the functioning of our society and that children learn using their senses. The audience agreed that children must come to school with the knowledge of what it feels, looks, and sounds like to be respectful of themselves and others, particularly their teachers and classmates.

We as a "learning community" (parents, teachers, administrators, and the public) learned together about recognizing and really internalizing for ourselves what respect looks like, feels like, and sounds like so that we can teach it first by example. We came away from the evening with a deeper understanding and mutual agreement of how respect is demonstrated and how to recognize when a child or ourselves crosses the line to disrespect.

If the topic of "respect" is your area of focus or interest, this is your opportunity to bring your views on the subject to the table, ask your questions, and share your thoughts on how best to accomplish the task of teaching respect universally within your community using the research base the experts provided and the available resources within your community. This provides the opportunity for an open exchange of ideas from the higher education institutions to the local district. It allows the experts the chance to transfer the knowledge produced from research to parents, school systems, and the community. The community gets to take part in the planning of the next necessary action, thus giving the plan a better chance of being successful.

The ideas discussed or plans decided on would be communicated to the part of the public that was not in attendance through a variety of ways. The research on the idea of respect and the argument of our expert in favor of it being a valued principle in the American education system would be presented in a way that all could understand.

This type of process helps in establishing guiding principles in our education system based on research and public input, helps shape our vision, and becomes self-perpetuating in that the knowledge originated in a higher education institution and, if the ideas meet public approval, they teach it to the next generation of teachers, counselors, and administrators. If we value an ideal or principle, it circles back into the teachers' curriculum. This is a vicious cycle, a process, in which we should want to get trapped.

The same process can be applied to concepts concerning teachers ready to teach. This time let's use the example of a principle that has been widely accepted already, or at least the terminology has: "high expectations for all students." The problem currently is that these are only words on paper until their application in our classrooms, homes, and communities is realized.

Those simple words, "high expectations for all students," are commonly seen in schools' vision or mission statements, or in state and national education propaganda. If the process described in the first example had been used, that complex concept of "high expectations for all students" would have been fully explained, the research presented to the public, and its significance to local curricula explored in depth by the stakeholders. Instead, it appears that "setting high expectations" has wrongly been put into practice by first laying out a list of knowledge standards. Then we expect the teacher to drill those into the student and expect the student to then perform their regurgitation ritual on tests. We call that "educational achievement."

The true complexity of expectations and their effect on students is explained in depth in *Reaching Higher: The Power of Expectations in Schooling* (Weinstein, 2002). It is a subject that is deserving of an evening lecture, especially since the impression is that the public and many educators do not understand what is at the heart of "high expectations." It is a topic that is useful for parents as well as teachers and has the potential to make a huge difference in people's lives.

For the purposes of this example, let's assume that no local expert was able to deliver the topic satisfactorily. Instead, we were able to get a faculty member from our local college to moderate discussion and provide an introduction of the topic. We had access to video conferencing that we used to connect to an expert in another part of the country who agreed to provide answers to our questions.

The introduction clarified the concept as something that is not necessarily a new one. Many an adult may remember as a child overhearing parents talking about their belief that, if you keep telling a child that they are "bad" and "will never amount to anything," the child starts to believe you and what you are saying more likely becomes a reality. In other words, what you are expecting to happen becomes the truth; it is the phenomenon of a "self-fulfilling prophesy." It has both positive and negative aspects. On the positive side, if you tell a child they are capable of accomplishing a task, it is more likely they can.

To apply this concept in a classroom setting, educators would need to be made aware of the verbal and nonverbal cues that we adults relay to kids. To utilize an example of a verbal cue, a situation that developed with one of my son's math teachers could be used. The teacher told him that he would "never be good at trigonometry." Some nonverbal examples would be putting young students into ability groups, especially when they are labeled as "high" and "low," or designated in any way that it can be deciphered by kids. Kids in the low group aren't expected to be able to accomplish the same work as those in the high group. Placement in special programs that everyone knows are for the "slow" kids is also a nonverbal cue, as is placement of "faster" kids who may get to go do something perceived by others as more interesting. Those faster kids can be looked at as more worthy. These nonverbal examples are getting at the very structure and content of what we teach (the curriculum). Children are made aware of their shortcomings by our actions and reactions to their work. Our actions in educational settings tell kids what we expect of them and that has an effect on their academic outcome.

The good news seems to be what they call "resilience pathways" for kids to avoid falling prey to negative self-fulfilling prophesies. With the help of my dad's old math books, just such a path for my son was provided. He was told that we didn't believe what the teacher said and thought instead that the problem was that the book he was given to use, and the way the teacher was teaching it, just wasn't jiving with the way he learns. We didn't do much. We showed him how the material was taught in the past; he did well in the class and the highest score on his ACT was in trigonometry. The expectation was that he could do it, and he did.

The effects that high academic expectations can have on students' educational outcomes would be impossible to fully evaluate in any type of humane research. The debate on the subject may continue. But ask yourself: Is there harm in creating what amounts to a positive nurturing learning environment where all children are provided challenging opportunities?

Shouldn't we want all children to be given the opportunity to demonstrate how high they can reach when we don't limit them by words or actions? If this is what we want, what we value, shouldn't we be working with our teacher preparation programs to ensure that the next generation of teachers fully comprehends the principles of high expectations and self-fulfilling prophesies? Wouldn't that prevent classroom problems in the future?

This subject of high expectations is as important for parents to learn about as it is the teachers. We need to be able to recognize when the educational system is not holding high expectations for our students, plus we need to become more sensitive to the cues we send to our own children at home. The understanding of the concept of high expectations needs to be spread throughout our communities.

In our hypothetical community, the teachers' and administrators' input to the coordinator included multiple requests for the topic of materials support to be brought to the community's attention. In this instance, the educators were specifically referring to the lack of science materials and hands-on opportunities for older students to apply relevancy to their education and for exposure to career opportunities.

For information on science materials support, we turn to neighboring states and other local districts that have science centers. Some of them have arranged for community volunteer organizations to help put together science kits for easy use in classrooms. Others have purchased kits and called on volunteers to help keep them in order or help with hands-on projects in their classrooms. Nonprofit and for-profit organizations are available to come and explain how they work and present choices so a community can determine what works best for them.

To convey the need for learning opportunities to the community, we need to look again at the schools referred to as the Met. At the Met, all students have opportunities to do internships based on their interests. Through his observations and experiences there, Eliot Levine got to see "hands-on" applied in a way much bigger than just in science classes. He made a statement in his book that really hits home at this moment in time. He said, "Learning through doing is as old as humanity. The artificial rift between classroom and hands-on learning is a modern invention whose fallout is becoming apparent" (2002, 43).

We can reverse the effects of that fallout and prevent the rift in the classrooms in the future if we bring to our own communities the information and the inspiration of those that have been successful in implementing community projects that hold students' interest and keep them in school. Community members need to be made aware of what they can do to help and they don't have to chart new territory to do it. Research can guide their actions.

Bringing research to the people for their use is a course of action that can be applied to the many teaching principles and basic beliefs in human behaviors that need to be examined in the process of deciding what we value in education. The point is to have you consider the process used to decide what we value, and how to use those valued principles in the formation of our goals.

This same process could be applied by the stakeholders at each school, keeping the developmental stage of the learners and their interests in mind. As you can see in the examples and the process that they were meant to demonstrate, their success depends on coordination, cooperation, and communication.

The Institute for Diffusion of Knowledge

Transfer of all information pertinent to our educational beliefs and principles is an essential piece in fostering informed decisions. Information must be communicated in understandable language to all parents and the general public alike. Yet nobody is accountable for that piece of the equation. It is essential that we use the facts to drive our sense of civic duty to provide a check and balance of the system. We the people cannot do our part in this republic without the facts. If elections are any indication, it should be painfully clear that getting and deciphering the facts has become too time-consuming for the working class. We need to insist on a better way. Knowledge should be the key to any responsible decision making we do. It is essential to the responsible use of the process that I have been describing. "The process" itself is extremely important. It is the democratic process.

Seymour Sarason asked, "How can we justify our belief in the democratic principle elsewhere and then go back entirely upon it when we come to education?" (1993, 121). If we are to be successful, we can't and we shouldn't continue this practice out of habit. That has been an act of irresponsibility on our part. It's time we changed. It is time we focused our attention responsibly on the children within the education system of the United States. And people must be given the information they need to do that.

We must also keep in mind that the downfall of a democracy can come about when the majority is wrong. It does happen; the majority may not always be right. That is why an open exchange of ideas becomes so important. It can allow the voice of reason to enter the debate, if people listen to one another. The Junto and the American Lyceum were designed to provide information and foster that exchange of ideas.

We don't have to reinvent the wheel to set in motion the communication component of the equation. We have an excellent adult education agency in place that could serve the function of continuing education for teachers, counselors, and administration and provide education on educational issues for parents and the community.

That agency prides itself on following these principles: (1) fostering cooperation between the funding of its programs and other aspects of its work, including cooperation with other existing organizations (such as parent and teacher organizations in this example), (2) always directing its programs based on stakeholder input (parents, children, teachers, administrators, and the greater community in this case), (3) providing programs that are research based, and (4) always evaluating its programs to provide accountability to its own system. That agency is the Cooperative Extension Services of our land grant university system. Couldn't a second American Lyceum be established within that system?

Many people wrongly think of the Cooperative Extension Service as an institution solely based on agricultural education. It's not and it should be the logical extension service for education, given its heritage going back to Benjamin Franklin's Junto. But my impression is that schools of education have chosen not to use this system.

It appears that many schools of education have chosen to remain within their own cult. For our education system to function like a system, people must lower their walls, come down from the ivory towers, and work together. The institutional or personal barriers that have been erected must come down. Higher education cannot act in isolation.

Remember the components of communication and cooperation? They represented the plus marks in the equation. They bind the elements of success together and they should bring the people together so that they can act as the catalyst for change. Each of us must realize what we need to do to foster understanding and the process of change itself.

All of this should sound very doable; it is. Most of it is just common sense. These aren't radical ideas. They even sound as if they are things that the established local education systems could do on their own, each in their own way. Perhaps parents and teachers, with the help of colleges and universities, could work out the solutions for themselves for their part of the equation. With guidance they could change themselves; that's reform. But the heavily entrenched educational bureaucracy and our current Congress are incapable of changing themselves. And we the people should not allow ourselves to be pacified by the promise of reform.

The promise now is "to close the achievement gap with accountability, flexibility, and choice, so that no child is left behind." Closing the achievement gap is the goal of NCLB, which the new administration is currently supporting and will be making only minor changes to. They have begun to use the law's original name of the Elementary and Secondary Education Act (ESEA). But reform by another name is still reform.

What we want to achieve still needs defining. How you achieve "accountability" through laws in a local control democratic system needs to be further contemplated and debated. "Flexibility" should not be of the law itself but in classroom instruction. And "choice" should not be looked to as the answer but rather just a temporary step in this change process.

As discussed in *Choice or Commonality*, if educational responsibility remains solely on the immediate family, "'choice' may take place in a world of insufficient numbers of quality schools, inadequate information about the stakes and alternatives, and large numbers of people unable to use the choice system effectively. This state of affairs means choice for some and not for others, and whether a child's educational needs are met will depend on her parents' ability to choose" (Minow, 1999, 551). Does that sound in keeping with the promise of equal opportunity?

For the "formula for success" to work, we must use our heads, our hearts, and our history. We must recognize what is reform and remember that it has been tried before, repeatedly, and with the same result of not changing the system, not completing the equation, and never, to date, reaching the goal of equal educational opportunity. We must resist our temptation to take the small, relatively easy pieces only and not tackle the bigger picture.

Where the Going Gets Tough

The toughest element to tackle within the formula for success is the "Materials to Do It." We looked at an easy example, without details, without looking at the bigger piece. This money issue most certainly: (1) requires the most effort from the public to provide that much-needed catalyst for change, (2) is the hardest concept to understand the complexity of, and (3) without a doubt is the most controversial.

The material support for education does come in many forms. Much of the support for education costs the system nothing, or little, if it is done in a spirit of cooperation with community members, nonprofits, or volunteer groups. Those things are totally dependent on community efforts. That support is of extreme importance, so I don't mean to slight it in any way but want to limit this discussion to governmental support for the material needs of schools.

In that context, materials support for education is financial support, is taxation, is supposed to be dealt with through representation, is married to politics, is directed by big business, and has failed our children. This is the part of the equation that continues to resist reform of any kind at the national level where it must start—but not with reform.

We must insist on revolutionizing our governing structure of education, from top to bottom, to provide us the freedom to adequately support our schools financially. Dysfunctional needs to become functional. Inefficient needs to become efficient. Ineffective needs to be eliminated. For this to happen, we the people must unite in a big way to be that much needed catalyst for real change. It is time we all, even our government, do what is right for the children of the United States.

We need to look at the governing structure of education, study it, research it, and present our findings to the public (just as we should with every philosophy and principle that we wish to establish). We must debate through an open exchange of ideas, but, then, we must end the debate and formulate our desires into a vision and plan.

If we can't come to a general consensus, we go back to the drawing board. The Founding Fathers laid out the Constitution of the United

States for us, but not without some difficulties. The obstacles didn't stop them. They prevailed. We can surely provide the needed change to our governing structure to ensure delivery of equal educational opportunities for our children now and for posterity.

Financial support for education should not be dependent on where you live. Financial support for education must become a national priority never again to be tampered with because of the cost of war. In the United States at this crucial moment in time, we can't afford to waste the potential talent of any of our children, rich or poor. Now let the controversy begin.

I understand that education is seen as a state responsibility, but I would argue that we need to examine how that came about and think about the current reality. The Founding Fathers did not include education as a fundamental right under the U.S. Constitution. Possibly by default, it is covered in the Tenth Amendment, which states, "The powers not delegated to the United States by the Constitution, nor prohibited by it to the States, are reserved to the States respectively, or to the people."

The Founding Fathers also did not give the U.S. Congress the power to legislate on the subject of education. They did give the Congress the authority to tax and spend for the general welfare and Congress has used that, in its application to education, irresponsibly. Also, consider an article on "Constitutional Requirements Governing American Education" (education.stateuniversity.com), which talks about a Supreme Court case and the agreement of many that "the content of education was a classic area of state, not federal authority." Yet we have been witness to and victims of Congress overstepping its authority by holding states hostage with the dangling of the carrot of money leading to intrusion into our classrooms. And we let it happen.

At a local school board meeting shortly after one of its members had been to our State School Board Association meeting, one thing that was brought back to the group was the idea that "we must align our curriculum to the test or there will be punitive damages." Our curriculum, what is being taught (the content) and how, is being decided based on fear and standardized test results rather than on what our community's children need from the education system. Our government was out of line with the No Child Left Behind law. Our government has not been kept in "check."

Federal funding has gone from recognition of the urgent needs of the impoverished children to testing and accountability and now is turning to improving the data systems. When will we learn that it is the story behind the numbers that needs our urgent and focused attention—it's the child in the seat? Building robust data systems is a luxury the cost of which can only be justified after teachers are given the classroom resources they need and the children are given the community resources they are lacking. Where is the "check and balance"?

As firmly as we believe in our individual states' rights and our local control of education, we must open our minds to the idea that we should and can maintain local control of our local schools curriculum (which we currently aren't doing) while insisting on our federal government functioning effectively to provide material support without interference in the classroom. I would argue that the law is on the side of this concept. I'll state it again. The U.S. Congress is authorized to tax and spend for the general welfare of its people. It is not authorized to intrude in the local control of curriculum content.

That does not mean we can't establish national values as our guides. As we develop our educational philosophies and principles, we can work side-by-side with financial analysts charting the essential materials needed and planning a smooth transition to federal financial support of quality educational opportunity for all schools throughout the United States.

Some may argue here that equality in funding has not lead to equality in educational opportunity. I agree. But we must get our minds around the idea that equality in funding is not the same as adequate funding. This is where we have to keep our goal in mind and be very careful not to take funding, as a separate entity, out of the equation for success. That may be where funding reforms have failed to demonstrate themselves as the "cure all" in providing better student outcomes.

It appears these reforms in funding didn't work in consort with defining equal opportunities for a quality education and what efforts that entails. In short, some schools require more effort and therefore more money to get them up to a satisfactory quality. Or we can look back at the ESEA of 1965 and follow its example of looking at money as aid to needy children versus the idea of aid to schools. In either case, NCLB results, if used properly and in conjunction with other statistics, should prove useful in identifying where to begin.

The biggest obstacle to adequately funding education at this moment in time may well be our climbing debt and looming financial devastation. On the other hand, the present is the time to invest in the future of our country and no better way exists than investing in education. It is education's time to rise up above the rubble that greed and ignorance has created. Will we stand united as a nation behind our children's future?

What Will It Take?

I've referred to revolutionizing the system but not really talked about the meaning of the word "revolution." One meaning is "a complete or radical change of any kind" (*Webster's*, 1976). But radical change is not desirable; complete change is essential to succeed. We know reforms have never fixed the system. We know they have improved one school at a time, but the process has never reached all children and these movements seem to always suffer setbacks. We know in our hearts that we need to make this change; we know where we can begin. But what will it take to move us?

There won't be a single event triggering this revolution in education. If that was going to happen, NCLB should have been that event. It should have triggered our modern-day Boston Tea Party. We should have been burning tests on our Capitol's steps. Instead, one consequence (intentional or unintentional) of NCLB was that it further fractured the people. NCLB appeared to be giving us the freedom as individual states to decide our standards and spend our money on designing and testing tests. But, in the end, we were trapped into setting our curriculum based on NCLB rules rather than the needs of our population of learners. It effectively divided the states with busy work at a time when we should have united against the intrusion of the federal government in our classrooms. Just as an administrator can choose to diffuse or ignore any single parent's concerns or issue without fixing the root of a problem, our governing structure in the education system has effectively subdued us with reforms and choice and successfully divided us with policy.

The time has come for all of us to realize that we must do what is right. We must make this a united effort, for division can surely bring us down. We must unite in our pursuit of the ideal of universal education promoted by George Washington. Equal educational opportunity is the right thing for America. We must realize that we need the common sense of ordinary Americans working within a framework of the democratic process to decide the right course. Then we need the people's persistence and vigilance to finally make our educational goals a reality in every classroom. Ask questions; get to the truth. Arm yourself with knowledge. These are your schools; you should have a say in the direction of change. Make your voice heard.

The choice is yours; what's next is up to you. History and the experience of others tell us that we must unite behind a common purpose to make our voices heard. Is there any more worthy common purpose than educating the next generation of our children? Shouldn't we arm them with the knowledge and skills they need to pursue their happiness and improve our democratic society?

> Democracy must be consciously promoted and transmitted to each new generation. The freedom of a democratic society enables the school to promote greater democracy and the society to improve education.

> John Dewey

CHAPTER EIGHT
DEMOCRACY AND EDUCATION

The great keep the poor from the knowledge of their rights; and it is knowledge alone, diffused through the whole body of the people, that can preserve them from tyranny.

John Adams

Parents can offer insight into how their child learns best. Parents want to have a say in how and what their child is taught. Teachers want to have a say in what and how they teach. Local economies must have a voice in letting their needs of the education system be known. None of these groups should be forced to accept what the government has decided for them, especially when the government's layers of bureaucrats have ignored and diluted our desires or just quit listening. This should not be happening in a democratic society. For either democracy or education to function as intended, we the people need to be informed and have a voice in the decision-making process, our democratic process.

The second paragraph of the Declaration of Independence begins with: "We hold these truths to be self-evident, that all Men are created equal, that they are endowed by their Creator with certain unalienable Rights, that among these are Life, Liberty, and the Pursuit of Happiness—That to secure these Rights, Governments are instituted among Men, deriving their just Powers from the Consent of the Governed." Think about those words. The power of government should come from the consent of the governed. And, to clarify education's link to democracy, here is the infamous quote from George Washington's Farewell Address to Congress: "Promote then, as an object of primary importance, institutions for the general diffusion of knowledge. In proportion as the structure of a government gives force to public opinion, it is essential that public opinion should be enlightened."

For strengthening our republic, or strengthening our education system, we continue to be missing an essential element in the experiment. Why?

Our Founding Fathers knew how important education would be to achieving a true functioning republic that would endure the test of time. H. G. Good summarized it best in writing that "the educational thinkers of the revolution and the following years" viewed education as "a means of preserving liberty, securing unity, promoting good citizenship and developing the resources of the land and people. Education would help maintain the union of states, a united people and a republican government" (1956, 81–82).

Unfortunately, our Founding Fathers didn't frame that education system for us. They left it for us to do. It is time we face that unmet challenge. Obstacles have been created by the modern economy, mobilization, globalization, and the resultant decline of the family structure and function. But Americans have overcome obstacles of the past that were far greater than that.

We need to awaken the spirit within us that has made America the great nation it has been. Americans not only successfully staged a revolution, settled a land, and established a new republic, Americans revolutionized the industrial world; we can revolutionize our own education system.

The foundation for our great country was set by the Declaration of Independence. Its writers anticipated the corruption and greed of the federal government, for they went on to say, in reference to life, liberty, and the pursuit of happiness, "that whenever any Form of Government becomes destructive of these Ends, it is the Right of the People to alter or to abolish it, and to institute new Government, laying its Foundation on such Principles, and organizing its Powers in such Form, as to them shall seem most likely to effect their Safety and Happiness." Our Founding Fathers were telling us that it is the people's right to make alterations to our government.

America is still known as "the land of opportunity." Education provides opportunities. It is an individual adult's responsibility to strive to be ever learning for the opportunity to improve their own life. It is their responsibility. A child's education is quite a different matter.

We as a nation have a responsibility to our children. When an educational plan for this country truly focuses responsibly on our children, our right to make alterations to our governing structure becomes not just a right, but our duty. For the United States to continue to be a land of opportunity, we must have an education system that provides an equal opportunity for quality education to all children, at all times, in peace or at war.

Change is never easy. Humans instinctively resist change. Our Founding Fathers indicated their understanding of this fact in the Declaration by writing that "Mankind are more disposed to suffer, while Evils are sufferable, than to right themselves by abolishing the Forms to which they are accustomed." They were speaking out to future generations, to us.

The ideals of democracy have not let down we the people of the United States; we the people have let down our republic. We need to listen to the words that were left to us, reflect, and respond. We must right ourselves, for we are riding on turbulent waters, teetering in our canoe, and holding on to the hope that we don't tip and go down.

As just a parent, I am powerless to change the flow of the current.

REFLECTIONS

Ideals are ideas about what should be; at the same time we know and regret that we will fall short of the mark. It is one thing to aim and fall short of the mark; it is inexcusable if knowing you will inevitably fall short of the mark, you do not even take aim.

Seymour B. Sarason

In our education system, good people are doing good things every day. But the system is not always good to them and they too can be left feeling powerless. When a teacher's obituary reads, "It was her wish that everyone could and should get a good education, but though she loved her students and colleagues, the pressures of the education system became something she no longer wanted to fight," that should give us pause.

Why does it seem like such a fight? Getting my children through school felt like a fight. It didn't have to be that hard. Maybe it was so hard because I never understood the fight, never knew the answer to the question: Who is my opponent? Who has been working against me in the battle to provide my children, and others, with the best education possible? I don't want to believe that it is racists and devious elitists who have continued this fight against equal educational opportunities for children. I don't want to believe that it is the ambivalence of the public in general that limits educational opportunities. I want to believe that "we know not what we do."

The absence of the democratic process in working through educational issues leads to frustration, decreased productivity, loss of liberty, and, in some cases, failure. It illustrates the failure to listen. It takes away the people's voice.

This book was written because of the fact that, as a parent, a taxpayer, and a citizen of the United States, I could find no other way to make my voice heard on educational issues, large or small. If local control is our guiding principle, we must understand that local control of education only works in education's favor within the framework of the democratic process and that only occurs when people listen to one another.

People must begin to think about the immeasurable results of cooperation. The productivity of people is improved in a positive work environment that applies to both teachers and their students alike. The chance for positive self-fulfilling prophesies to become realities is increased. And when parents become welcomed into the equation for success and share the vision of their children's schools, what kind of multiplying effect does that have on positive student outcomes?

Many parents, including myself, have been seen in a bad light. I can't help but wonder how different it might have been had I been given the chance within this public school system to participate in helping plan my own children's education like they do at the Met. I wonder how it would feel to know my children were going daily to a school with a strong sense of cooperation and respect for all, like at Central Park East.

More than anything, I wanted to see my schools consistently reinforce some of the things I value: respect, honesty, fairness, healthy habits, and acceptance of others, including their views. I wanted my schools to be places where people genuinely cared about one another and every child's learning opportunities.

David Bensman stressed that schools are about more than just academic development; they're about how "social and emotional development grows out of caring relationships, relationships between one whole human being and another" (2000, 127). Children want us to care. Unfortunately, caring people too many times find that passion, knowledge, experience, common sense, and even wisdom may not be enough to improve educational opportunity. And improve it we must, for with every day we are wasting time, money, energy, talent, and resources in moving toward an educational goal that we the people have not set.

No longer can we continue to undereducate our people if we wish to survive in an economy reliant on an educated workforce. Education is em powering. Education promotes change. Education is central to the solutions of all our social ills because it is the essential infrastructure underlying all social improvement. Our society needs to alter the structure of education and lay new foundation based on principles in which we believe.

It is time for a revolution, but not one that tears down a government—rather, one that builds up a strong education system with the capacity to supply the next generation of workers, scholars, and politicians prepared to take on the challenges of tomorrow, whatever they may be. We mustn't settle with the dysfunctional bureaucracy that we currently refer to as our education system.

That bureaucracy could have done better by my own children. Fortunately, individual teachers along the way helped make my children the successes they are despite the shortcomings of their K–12 education. I did fail to get them the best. But they did not fail; they didn't get left behind because of the caring, competent individuals in their lives and in their classrooms. It has always been a teacher that makes the difference in education—always will be. And I apologize for referring to any school as a "failed" school. No school is a total failure when we have people in it that care.

The problems in education have always been the same—how to deal with discipline, how to provide quality teachers, better working conditions, and adequate pay, and how to stimulate public interest in education and its financial support. The answers have always been the same—educate parents and children about the rules of a civil society, better educate teachers and administrators, including about the community resources available to help them and their students, and educate the public with the facts. After that, it becomes the public's duty to act responsibly.

Nothing is in place to ensure that good practices can't go by the wayside with changing administration. It is a fact that nothing is in place to maintain balance in this ever-changing current of public education, except perhaps our sorely ignored laws. Through understanding, we must be the ones to add the missing ingredient.

It's not immediate investment in new assessments and accountability systems that we require. It is investment in "ensuring that teachers have the world's best training and preparation." It's not "incubators of innovation" that we so desperately need; we need caring individuals with the ability to listen and individualize instruction (White House—Press Office Fact Sheet: Expanding the Promise of Education in America). In Idaho, our law governing schools ends by saying "Fulfillment of the expectations of a thorough system of public schools will continue to depend upon the vigilance of district patrons, the dedication of school trustees and educators, the responsiveness of state rules, and the meaningful oversight by the legislature" (Idaho Code 33-1612).

If we continue to believe that accountability will come about through laws, we are missing the whole concept of local control and the democratic process. We continue to use the law to try to achieve accountability and improve learning while, at this moment in time, we would be wise to use our understanding of what it is we want and need to do.

No matter which side of the many warring political factions you belong on, one aspect in a democracy on which we can agree is the fact that informed citizenry is necessary to give accountability to any plan involving our public institutions. We say we believe in local control, but we don't give the local people the information they need to lend an informed voice to the debate, if they had a voice. Like the balance in our republic between power and privilege, balance within the public education system is in the hands of the people. Vigilance by the people remains inconsistent and unpredictable. Equal opportunity under those circumstances remains a distant dream.

H. G. Good wrote about a time in the colonial days before our government was firmly established when men became obsessed with the fear that time was "running out," that it was "a race between education and catastrophe" (1956, 93). That time, liberty prevailed. It was a time when the educated class ruled based on its wisdom and virtues. True statesmen governed. Today, we should be very worried.

We people want to find the easy way out. We want someone else to take care of the problems for us. But neither a democracy nor a republic works and survives based on that pretense. The final plan to establish a universally fair education system in America must not be someone else's plan or that of just one person.

Muriel Lester provided an example of a time and a place where the young people were restlessly waiting for their rulers to come up with a plan. When a leader finally stepped up with a strict, very detailed plan, they followed him in droves. That time was the 1930s, that place was Europe, and that leader was Hitler. Let's look ahead and choose not to go down that path, ever.

People have from time to time rallied around the cause of equal educational opportunity. Plans were made. But time and again our vigilance wanes; our failure to see our plans through has been of our own doing. Our country's repeated pattern of going to war has derailed many plans and the establishment of adequate financial support for education. The dream of educational opportunity in the Great Society has not come close to a reality. Education has suffered terribly from the collateral damages of wars. And we lack strong leadership on the issue.

You, the professors and researchers in education and other relevant related fields, have the knowledge we the people need to finally establish our governing principles and philosophies upon which the United States will provide equal educational opportunity. The people must be given that knowledge; the people must then take back their voice and lead.

Many stand up to be counted as national leaders but currently in this country we lack ample leadership with vision and integrity. Our government appears to no longer be run by men and women with virtue and wisdom; it appears to be run by those that tout their party line. Strong leaders have not been vocal enough in any recent attempt to improve education or even bring the subject into a national debate. Education is the nonpartisan issue.

The fact that heated debate about education is not occurring on the political front doesn't mean it shouldn't. It doesn't mean that everything is fine; it's not. The lack of debate shows that we have leaders without a clear vision for the future of American education. They have no worthy plans for education to debate. We have a unique opportunity to shape their plan.

This election cycle, the people were voicing their desire for change. Meanwhile, the political battle in Washington, D.C., continued to be framed as the beliefs of our Founding Fathers versus entitlements, the right versus the left, while the real battle for the common people remains that of the pursuit of happiness and the American Dream; the disconnect is huge. We must bridge that gap through education and an exchange of ideas. Collectively, we have the answers to once again find balance. If we can overcome our failure to listen to one another, we can maintain balance while revolutionizing our education system. In *A Peacock in the Land of Penguins*, BJ Gallagher and Warren H. Schmidt make the point that the "land of opportunity" "is more than a place. . . . It is a state of mind . . . an attitude. It is an openness to new ideas, a willingness to listen, an eagerness to learn, a desire to grow, and the flexibility to change."

Change at this point in our history is essential to our survival as a republic. We must develop a functioning education system without political influence that can truly provide an equal opportunity to quality education. We can develop that system to be, once again, based on trust in the fact that we will seek fairness and balance in our decisions for the future. Revolutionary change is necessary because the pressing issues in education need to be faced with a determination to make the change real and lasting by changing the very core of our system so that we don't keep repeating a history not worth repeating. This time, let's not quit with the job unfinished, the plan unfulfilled.

Muriel Lester dedicated *Dare You Face Facts?* "to the common people by whose sweat our grain is produced, our livestock tended, our houses built, our cloths made, our furnaces stoked, our factories manned, and who keep the world sane" (1940). I am asking fellow parents, educators, and all citizens of the United States to please stop the insanity of repeated failures and their detriment to our children.

We must have faith in the initiative, resourcefulness, and ability of the people of the United States to unite for the common good. It should be through the idea of "one kid at a time" that we provide educational opportunity. We just can't continue at the pace of one school at a time and expect that we'll ever float this stream to its fruition.

No Child Left Behind identified some schools truly in need of immediate help. Don't go rushing into those schools without a plan established through the democratic process. Don't demonstrate the workings of a pendulum, again. Instead, consider inching to the center and, together, see through to the end the changes that are necessary in the establishment of a balanced education system. That system, and the country in general, is in serious trouble and the very basis of democracy itself is our saving grace. The balance is in our hands.

Let's make fixing our struggling schools a priority, for within them are children that need us to do that. Address the issues of the communities that have created those schools, for they are failing families and children in other ways. Make the focus our children, all our children. Use a guiding plan that defines high expectations for all the participants, including our expectations of our government's role in education: "Ultimately, it is a collective responsibility to ensure that no one is abandoned . . . to a dead-end, dismal school" (Minow, 1999, 555).

I am not your average parent only because I made the choice to go beyond what was expected of me. We must go beyond what has routinely been expected of us. And as we move forward in creating good precedents, let us always remember to look back and follow the wise beliefs and principles that have been laid down before us, many in education laws or other documents. We can build a new American education system in the true sense of the word "system."

We would do well to begin by looking back upon the premise, the belief, on which the 1965 education law was based; children living in poverty in the United States deserve education at a level equal to those more fortunate. At that time, our union in their wisdom recognized they must supply the necessary funding and services to provide that equality.

At this point, I firmly believe there is not a single idea within this book that we cannot implement. That is a fact. That's being a realist. I'm also an optimist, but even a true optimist has moments of uncertainty. I confess to a feeling that has loomed over me like a huge, stormy cloud of doubt. I couldn't put my finger on it until the day I was permitted to attend my daughter's high school political philosophy class.

I was stunned to speechlessness when I heard this young woman of mine state her thesis as "morality has gone from a universal idea to extremely relative." My translation in relation to today's society and my own dilemma over doubts is what is right and wrong has gone from knowing what is right for the common good to evaluating what is right relative to what "I" gain.

I know equality in education is right for the common good. I do not know with certainty what the majority thinks is right for the education of American children. Do we value equality in education? Do we value education? Do we care at all? My great uncertainty can only be answered by the people. Will we stand together united as a nation, not this time behind a war but behind our children? Will we make certain that we pass on to our children a more perfect union? Let us ensure the promise by promoting the proper and necessary education of all the people of our nation.

As a parent that cares, I end with sadness in my heart for all those children that are not as fortunate as my own. It is a sadness that will stay with me until the day our society knows with confidence that all students have been given the educational background to make informed, wise choices that contribute to the functioning of a democratic society. That sadness will remain in my heart until the day we, as a nation, can say with assurance that we are doing our very best to provide all children with the opportunity to reach their potential through their encounter with competent, caring individuals within their communities and the public education system of the United States.

As just a parent, my time in the K–12 system has ended with the belief of a brighter future for education still springing forth from my heart. I have many hopes. I hope you understand and see the power in understanding. I hope you see the answers have surfaced, again. I hope you are disturbed that the answers are within reach and uncomfortable with the fact that we haven't snatched them from the stream and clung to them like our lives, our children's lives, depended on it. I hope, in your heart, that you know the answer. The answer is us.

My vision for the education of the citizens of the United States is to see the people unite behind the ideal of equal opportunity. I see an awakening of the American spirit. I see us take aim. I see my stormy cloud of doubts bursting open, this time with kept promises that quickly send us down the turbulent stream to calmer waters.

> In the evolutionary stream we have to keep adjusting ourselves to changing environment. We have to be often disturbed, made uncomfortable: otherwise we should be content with second best.
>
> Muriel Lester

BIBLIOGRAPHY

Barr, Robert D., and William H. Parrett. *Hope Fulfilled for At-Risk and Violent Youth: K–12 Programs That Work*, second ed. Needham Heights, MA: Allyn & Bacon, 2001.

Bensman, David. *Central Park East and Its Graduates: "Learning by Heart."* New York: Columbia University, Teachers College Press, 2000.

Bradbury, Ray. *Fahrenheit 451*, second ed. New York: Del Rey Book, 1953.

Congressional Quarterly. *Congress and the Nation*: *A Review of the Government and Politics During the Johnson Years*, vol. II, 1965–1968. Washington, DC: Congressional Quarterly, 1969.

Cooperative Study of Secondary School Standards. *Evaluation of Secondary Schools: General Report on the Methods, Activities, and Results of the Cooperative Study of Secondary School Standards*: Author, Washington, DC, 1939.

Encyclopedia Americana International Edition, volume 17. Danbury, CT: Grolier, 1999.

Gallagher, BJ, and Warren H. Schmidt. *A Peacock in the Land of Penguins: A Story about Courage in Creating a Land of Opportunity*. Naperville, IL: Simple-Truths, 2008.

Good, H. G. *A History of American Education*, first ed. New York: The Ohio State University, Macmillan, 1956.

Hamilton, Alexander, Madison, James, Jay, John. *The Federalist Papers*, 1787-1788. Introduction by Garry Wills, 1982. New York: Bantam Dell, 2003.

Hofstradter, Richard. *The Age of Reform: From Bryan to F.D.R.* New York: Vintage, 1955.

Hubbard, L. Ron. *Learning How to Learn*. Los Angeles: Bridge Publication, 1992.

Idaho Code Commission. *Idaho Code containing the General Laws of Idaho Annotated*, Titles 33-34. Charlottesville, VA: Michie, 2008.

Lester, Muriel. *Dare You Face Facts?*, third ed. New York: Harper & Brothers Publishers, 1940.

Levine, Eliot. *One Kid at a Time: Big Lessons from a Small School*. New York: Columbia University, Teachers College Press, 2002.

Loucks-Horsley, Susan. *The Concerns-Based Adoption Model (CBAM): A Model for Change in Individuals*. Dubuque, IA: Kendall/Hunt Publishing, 1996.

Minow, Martha. "Choice or Commonality: Welfare and Schooling after the End of Welfare as We Knew It." *Duke Law Journal* 49 (1999): 493–559.

Payne, Ruby K. *Working with Parents: Building Relationships for Student Success*, second ed. Highlands, TX: aha! Process, 2005.

Phillips, Kevin. *Arrogant Capital: Washington, Wall Street, and the Frustration of American Politics*. New York: Little, Brown & Co., 1994.

Sacks, Peter. *Standardized Minds: The High Price of America's Testing Culture and What We Can Do to Change It*. Cambridge, MA: Perseus Books, 1999.

Sarason, Seymour. *The Case for Change: Rethinking the Preparation of Educators*. San Francisco: Jossey-Bass Publishers, 1993.

———. *Parental Involvement and the Political Principle: Why the Existing Governance Structure of Schools Should be Abolished*. San Francisco: Jossey-Bass Publishers, 1995.

Slosson, Edwin E. *The American Spirit in Education*. New Haven, CT: Yale University Press, 1921.

"Smith-Towner Bill." *The Elementary School Journal* (April 1920): 575–83.

Valverde, G., and W. Schmidt. "Refocusing U.S. Math and Science Education." *Issues in Science and Technology* (Winter 1997–1998): 60–66.

Webster's New World Dictionary, second college ed. Cleveland, OH: William Collins + World Publishing, 1976.

Weinstein, Rhona. *Reaching Higher: The Power of Expectations in Schooling*. Cambridge, MA: Harvard University Press, 2002.

White House—Press Office Fact Sheet. "Expanding the Promise of Education in America." March 10, 2009. www.whitehouse.gov/the_press_office/Fact-Sheet-Expanding-the-Promise-of-Education-in-America/.

NOTEWORTHY PEOPLE

Throughout this book each quotation used at chapter and section beginnings was carefully chosen to convey a thought. Many of the people quoted may not be familiar to you at all or as contributors to educational improvement. Many have gone to their graves with unfulfilled dreams for improved educational opportunity. They all deserve another look and merit another listen.

As with any attempt at giving a reader a historical perspective, the following brief descriptions are skewed based on my perspective and what I would like the reader to take away from this section. I encourage all to explore further and read works by these people or what others have written about them. Their individual and combined contributions to education and the world in general are truly inspiring.

The majority of facts were gathered from the 2002 *World Book Encyclopedia* published by World Book, Inc. out of Chicago, Illinois. Other quotes or additional facts were found within articles as indicated.

I encourage the reader to take the time to refer back in the book to the quotes as indicated before reading about each person. It adds depth to the understanding of their words.

John Adams (1735–1826)

See quotation on page 117

John Adams was a Harvard College graduate who taught school briefly before going on to practice law. He bravely and openly opposed the Stamp Act and was said to have become "enraged" about the British tax on tea, thus becoming infamous for his role in adoption of the Declaration of Independence. As a delegate to the Second Continental Congress in 1776, he urged Thomas Jefferson to be the one to draft that document for us.

About education, he wrote, "Laws for the liberal education of youth, especially of the lower class of people, are so extremely wise and useful, that, to a humane and generous mind, no expense for this purpose would be thought extravagant" (www.liberty1.org/John Adams Thoughts on Government.htm).

Francis Bacon (1561–1626)

See quotation on page 57

Francis Bacon was born in London, entered Trinity College, Cambridge, at the age of twelve, and held several government positions. He believed that, to discover truths, the mind must be rid of four prejudices: (1) tribe—the tendency to generalize (uncritical perception cannot be trusted); (2) cave—the tendency to base knowledge on experiences, education, and tastes (failing to see the variables in these things); (3) marketplace—the tendency to depend on language to communicate (words may be misinterpreted); and (4) theater—the tendency to be influenced by previous philosophies and laws of reasoning that are merely products of imagination.

His greatest contribution to education and science in particular was the development of the scientific method of solving problems: "He argued that a clear system of scientific inquiry would assure man's mastery over the world" (www.blupete.com).

Nicholas Murray Butler (1862–1947)

See quotation on page 69

Butler is known as an educational administrator, national Republican leader, advisor to seven presidents, and university president. He received his bachelor's, master's, and doctoral degrees from Columbia College (University).

He established the institution known as Teachers College, became president of Columbia University in 1902, founded the *Educational Re-*

view, served on the New Jersey Board of Education, and was instrumental in the development of the College Entrance Examination Board. Theodore Roosevelt referred to him as Nicholas Miraculous Butler.

Butler "sought to unite the world of education and that of politics in a struggle to achieve world peace through international cooperation." He won the Nobel Peace Prize along with Jane Addams in 1931 (Nobelprize.org).

Calvin Coolidge (1872–1933)

See quotation on page 87

Calvin Coolidge served as vice president under Warren Harding and became our thirtieth president on Harding's death. Coolidge then won the following election and was viewed as very popular with the people of that time.

He felt education was "primarily a means of establishing ideals" and that its "first great duty is the formation of character, which is the result of heredity and training." In his view, "the whole question at issue is, what does the public welfare require for the purpose of education? What are the fundamental things that young Americans should be taught? What is necessary for society to come to a larger comprehension of life?" (community.middlebury.edu).

John Dewey (1859–1952)

See quotations on pages 92 and 116

A graduate of the University of Vermont, with a Ph.D. from Johns Hopkins, John Dewey left his mark on the world as an educator, philosopher, and leader of the pragmatism movement. During his career, he lectured throughout the world and here at home on various issues from education to political and social movements, including women's suffrage.

His own philosophy has been labeled as instrumentalism, in that he believed we must use intelligence as an instrument for overcoming obstacles. A focus of his writings was often on the problem of how to close the gap between thought and action. He thought children coming to school should be considered in the context that they are "to do things and live in a community which gave them real, guided experiences which fostered their capacity to contribute to society" (wildercom.com).

Christopher Dock (late 1690s–1771)

See quotation on page 58

Christopher Dock immigrated to the United States around 1714. He was seen as a deeply religious person and served as a schoolmaster for Mennonite schools in Skippack and Philadelphia. He is credited with writing what is considered the first American book of teaching (pedagogy) and also one on etiquette called *A Hundred Rules of Conduct for Children*.

Here is an excerpt from that book: "Toward your fellows act lovingly and peacefully; do not quarrel with them, hit them, dirty their clothes with your shoes or ink, nor give them nicknames. Act toward them always as you would have them act towards you" (www.skippack.org).

Ralph Waldo Emerson (1803–1882)

See quotations on pages 41 and 71

Emerson is remembered as a philosopher and literary artist. Due to his family history and social position, Emerson entered Harvard at the age of fourteen. He taught school briefly before returning to school himself to study theology. He was ordained a Unitarian pastor and served as such for several years.

In 1833, he began his career as a lecturer, which included time on the Chautauqua Circuit for which the American Lyceum was the forerunner. In a speech of his at Harvard in 1837, Emerson "challenged his audience to cease imitating Europe and to ground their ideas in American resources, sincerity and realism." "Self-Reliance" was one of his more noteworthy themes and, in his terms, "to be self-reliant was to listen to and heed the still, small voice of God within" (www.25.uua.org).

H. G. Good (1880–1971)

See quotations on pages 61, 68, and 74

In an article published in *School and Society* ("The Approach to the History of Education," vol. XX, no. 504, August 23, 1924, 231–37), Good talks about approaching the history of education in relation to teacher preparation. He states, "Probably, as is now widely believed, young persons preparing to become teachers should first be introduced to some of the concrete problems of their profession."

He felt we were approaching teacher training by teaching "them their trade." And he suggested "if our purpose were—as it should be—the stimulation of professional intelligence we should undertake the task of cultivating a seriously critical attitude toward education." He advised that "[w]hat we ought to do depends upon what we mean to accomplish through the means at our command."

John F. Kennedy (1917–1963)

See quotation on page 70

John F. Kennedy was elected as our thirty-fifth president with the campaign pledge to "get America moving again." He launched economic programs to do just that while also responding to the demand for equal rights in the United States, the need for human rights throughout the world, and the call for stopping the spread of nuclear weapons.

On June 11, 1963, with the Alabama National Guard ready if needed, two young black men were peacefully admitted on the University of Alabama campus. In an address to the nation that night, Kennedy wisely stated that "law alone cannot make men see right." He went on to say, "A great change is at hand, and our task, our obligation, is to make that revolution, that change, peaceful and constructive for all." He asked for our help "to give a chance for every child to be educated to the limit of his talents" (www.americanrhetoric.com).

Martin Luther King Jr. (1929–1968)

See quotation on page 97

Dr. King was a Baptist minister and credited for being the main leader of the civil rights movement during the 1950s and 1960s. His "March on Washington" in 1963 was organized to urge Congress to pass John F. Kennedy's civil rights bill calling for equal opportunity in employment and education.

He left us many words worth contemplating, including from his Nobel Peace Prize acceptance speech in 1964: "I refuse to accept the idea that man is mere flotsam and jetsam in the river of life unable to influence the unfolding of events which surround him"; and from his sermon on April 3, 1968, "Let us move on in these powerful days, these days of challenge to make America what it ought to be. We have an opportunity to make America a better nation" (www.thekingcenter.org).

Muriel Lester (1883–1968)

See quotation on page 128

Muriel Lester has been labeled a social reformer, pacifist, and nonconformist (www.en.wikipedia.org). She was born into a wealthy, prominent English Baptist family but chose, instead of a Cambridge education, to devote her life to social justice by attempting to impact the structures of society through her Christian beliefs.

Lester seemed driven by the belief that we should take the teachings of Jesus Christ and apply them to daily life, especially in their application to the problems of the poor. In one poverty-stricken area of London, she and her sister Doris founded a community center they named Kingsley Hall in honor of their brother, whose estate provided the money needed to establish the center. It provided various services to the people including nondenominational spiritual guidance.

In the face of World War I and the call for patriotism of the English, Lester clung to her pacifist beliefs and joined the Fellowship of Reconciliation in 1914. She continued her work through politics and community organizing efforts and developed a following as a writer. In 1933, she became the ambassador of sorts for the international chapter of the fellowship and completed nine world trips on her speaking tour. That, of course, included the United States, where at least a good share of *Dare You Face Facts?* was written as World War II was mounting.

She was "detained" on returning to the British territories but on release returned to her work by organizing food and medical aid for Europeans on both sides of the issue. In a paper titled *A Random Chapter in the History of Nonviolence* by Michael L. Westmoreland-White, he wrote, "We can take strength from the way she faced her challenges as we face ours" (www.ecapc.org).

Horace Mann (1796–1859)

See quotation on page 93

The "Father of American Public School Education," Horace Mann, is credited with helping to establish a state-supervised, state-funded, mandatory-attendance school system in the United States. It has been said that one belief that motivated him to pursue that course was the idea that too much local control would result in improper schooling for some.

Mann also emphasized teacher training and established the first state-supported normal school (teacher training school) in 1839. Horace Mann understood the importance of money in making improvements to education and believed, among other things, that compensated school committees were needed to supervise teaching improvements and that it was in the best interest of businesses to pay taxation for education since they would most benefit.

In 1853 he became president of Antioch College in Ohio. In an address to graduates of that college a few weeks before he died, he said, "Be ashamed to die before you have won some battle for humanity" (www.cals.ncsu.edu).

Thomas Paine (1737–1809)

See quotation on page 99

Paine held a variety of jobs including one as a school teacher in London. As luck would have it, he met Benjamin Franklin, who helped him make his way to America, where he began a new career as a journalist in Philadelphia. He published *Common Sense*, the pamphlet that earned him the description as an agitator or revolutionary propagandist. He did not participate in reform measures themselves. His writings were his greatest accomplishments.

Paine left for Europe in 1787 and spent his time in France and Britain. It is said that his greatest work was *Rights of Man*, in which he "argued rationally that all men had an equal claim to political rights and that government must rest on the ultimate sovereignty of the people" (www.thehistoryguide.org).

William Penn (1644–1718)

See quotation on page 1

William Penn was expelled from England's Oxford University for rebelling against the rule that all enrolled students would attend the Church of England. He was later imprisoned several times for his preaching of

Quakerism, but was granted permission to govern an area of America due to his father being an admiral in good standing.

In his colony, he framed a government where the people could follow their religious beliefs without fear. Penn modeled the behavior he felt we should demonstrate toward each other, as evident by the way he got along with the Indians and honored any agreement he made with them. He did return to England, and it is said that two of his greatest works were a plan for a league of nations and an explanation of the principles for proper living.

Seymour B. Sarason (1919–)

See quotations on pages ix and 121

Dr. Sarason received his Ph.D. in psychology in 1942 and spent most of his career serving at Yale University in the fields of psychology and education. His many publications cover a wide range of topics. Particularly notable are his views on the multitude of "superficial" educational reforms and their failures.

Among his many awards is the Kappa Delta Pi Laureate in the field of education. During that society's 1999 convocation, Dr. Sarason was interviewed by Grant E. Mabie. Within that interview, he once again demonstrated the courage of his bluntness with words deserving of our reverence.

In talking about educators being treated with distain within the professional community, he said, "I'm being blunt, because people in positions to change this situation are not listening." He went on to say, "We need to move beyond predicting change to making it happen." He predicted that "only through shared knowledge of measurable results do we have any chance of truly making a difference, and, so far, no one is really trying to do that" (www.kdp.org).

Edward Austin Sheldon (1823–1897)

See quotation on page 66

While working as an evangelical missionary, Sheldon became interested in the education of the poor of Oswego. It's believed he had a genuine desire to make free education available to all children even though his work was later viewed as having significant underlying religious motivations to convert Catholic children to Protestantism. He proposed taxation of the public to form city-wide free schooling for Oswego unsuccessfully the first time but returned to that battle and eventually prevailed.

In a June 7, 2001, independent study done by Michael Ruddy while at the University at Buffalo, he discusses the philosophies of Thomas Jefferson and the actions of Sheldon with respect to the ideals of democracy and education and the separation of church and state. Ruddy states that "Jefferson's ideals of a public school system serving the democratic needs of the republic would eventually evolve into being, it would happen only by a means Jefferson would not have likely approved" (Oswego.edu/~ruddy/BuffaloPapers/OswegoinEducation/SheldonPaper.pdf).

Edwin E. Slosson (1865–1929)

See quotation on page 89

Edwin Emery Slosson received his B.S and M.S. from the University of Kansas and his Ph.D. from the University of Chicago. He taught chemistry at the University of Wyoming and was a chemist at the Wyoming Agricultural Experiment Station. He became an editor for *The Independent* and a published author of books and articles in both the field of science and literature (www.en.wikipedia.org).

In an introduction he wrote for *The Life Stories of Undistinguished Americans*, you get a sense for the way he combines science with literature and an understanding of how children learn when he states that "the hardest part of the training of the scientist is to get back the clear sight of his childhood." He goes on to talk about "the discovery of the importance of the average man" and how "it is the undistinguished people who move the world, or who prevent it from moving" (www.brocku.ca).

George Washington (1732–1799)

See quotation on page 85

George Washington earned the title of "Father of the Country" by serving as the commander of the Continental Army that won our independence, the presiding president of the convention that produced our constitution, and the first president of the United States. He believed in a strong national government and governed with a fairness and integrity that set the standard for all presidents to follow. He felt that he was dispensable and asserted that liberty was larger than any individual.

He did not attend college or learn a foreign language as was common among the "learned" men of that time. On his own, he read and studied and it is said that his library was quite extensive. It has been speculated that, because he felt his own education had been lacking, he "strongly believed in the value of a good education and left money in his will for establishing a school in Alexandria, Virginia as well as for establishing a national university."

According to an article by Jack D. Warren Jr., George Washington wrote, "It should be the highest ambition of every American to extend his views beyond himself and to bear in mind that his conduct will not only affect himself, his country, and his immediate posterity; but that its influence may be co-extensive with the world, and stamp political happiness or misery on ages yet unborn" (www.mountvernon.org).

ORGANIZATIONS WITH THE POTENTIAL TO HELP SCHOOLS BECOME BETTER

The organizations with the potential to help are as plentiful and varied as the unique issues that communities face.

So, to begin to examine different organizations, I looked first to some that I had looked at in the past. The work began by making phone calls to some whose numbers were readily available. By the end of that first morning, I felt a familiar frustration welling up in me. It was the same feeling I had experienced when doing research for the Safe Schools grant.

The sources of my frustration are the mounds of potentially useful knowledge, the amount of time it takes to explore the options, and the dead ends that you reach when you find organizations that sound good but no real person ready to help plot a working course of action. Also, the struggle continues with the idea that regardless of so many capable organizations willing and able to help, the fight to improve schools trudges on so slowly. With so many K–12 schools in the United States experiencing high drop-out rates, the question of the effectiveness of the existing organizations persists. I have to remind myself that the problem is not them; it is us. It's not that they didn't do their jobs; it's that we didn't do ours. We must make the assumption that they are capable of doing more, if we also do more.

The process of finding the best improvement options for the particular needs of any given community of learners could easily turn into a full-time job. To ask local volunteers alone to be responsible for a thorough review of research and information, and have the follow through necessary to sustain the human enthusiasm required to see through the completion of the change process, is asking for repeated setbacks or failures. Consider a community education coordinator to assist.

Changes based on the needs of the schools and their community requires the input necessary to decide the direction of improvements. If you look at most communities, this type of information has probably been collected from time to time in various ways and would make a useful starting point. This should not be about forgetting the past and starting over; it should be a process that reviews where a community has been, where it currently is, and where it needs to go. Then the real work begins.

Since most communities do not have a person available, qualified, or trained to act in the position of an education coordinator, if you are serious about improving the education in your own community, you can begin now. Start, as suggested earlier, by writing down what you think of as your goals for the education system, or your community in general. Look first in your own community as to what is already available in line with your goals. Joining the efforts that others are already making may prove rewarding. If you have not tried working with your local school district first, you should. Not all administrators are created equally; not all school boards are created equally. You may find your district, in earnest, is trying to take steps to improve. In that case, if they are sincere, they should welcome your involvement and appreciate your input even if and when you have a view different from their own. They should encourage you to join in their efforts and encourage others to join you. That effort can be fostered with the help of organizations such as those described under the "Parent and Community Participation" section.

District administration should be willing to answer any and all questions that you have. They should unconditionally give you the necessary facts. They should be able to provide facts that demonstrate whether or not it is your perception that your schools need improvement or if in fact they do. You should easily be able to make comparisons to neighboring schools, other states, and world standings. You should be able to look at and compare other indicators of healthy communities such as adult literacy.

Before you start the change process, you have to know what hard facts you are working toward improving. If they honestly don't have the facts, don't have a clear goal, or don't seem to know what resources are available to help them, organizations such as those listed under "Assessment" may be able to assist in finding the answers that are needed as a starting place.

Any single assessment of student achievement or any single source of information should not be used alone to draw conclusions from or determine direction. The sheer amount of statistics available is mind-boggling and the complication of political influence over the information makes it essential that all information be viewed critically.

Look back at your goal and decide specifically what facts would be necessary in monitoring progress toward your goal and determining when it has been reached. Consider your sources and what stake they may have in the outcome. And when you find conflicting "facts," you may have to rely on common sense or even instinct.

There is a very good chance that, as you begin to critically evaluate the resources available in your area, you will find others with similar goals, views, and desires for relevant, responsible improvement. It is the coordination of these efforts that hopefully proves very rewarding.

Appraisal of schools and communities that have already banded together to create or change schools to meet their children's needs can prove helpful. The "Schools that Make a Difference" section showcases organizations that may be able to help you develop similar schools if and when you are to the point that you have a broad base of community consensus to move forward.

Listed below are examples of organizations that can help. They are meant to be just that, examples. The selections I've made in this section are not made because of exhaustive research and a determination that these are the best. I can't make that determination for your community. I can only present ideas to show how you might go about school improvement.

You may want to also look at the publication of the Indicators Project 2002 titled "Strong Neighborhoods, Strong Schools," the link for which can be found at www.researchforaction.org. The article does a good job of clarifying the community/schools connection to improvement and may provide you with ideas about how other communities have approached school improvements through community organizing efforts.

Don't be afraid that you don't have the skills that you think you should to make a stand for your beliefs and the betterment of your community's children. When you approach school improvement with the willingness to listen to others and your work is driven from the heart, confidence in yourself and your abilities follows. The strongest element of change is the true desire to do what is right. If you have that, others can help.

ADDENDUM 2

Assessments

Communities That Care

When you look into information about this program, don't be fooled by the fact that it is under the direction of the Substance Abuse and Mental Health Services Administration (SAMHSA). This prevention program was developed by J. David Hawkins and Richard F. Catalano many years ago and its intentions were aimed at reducing and preventing youth crime and antisocial behavior, drug (including alcohol) abuse, school failure, and school-age pregnancy.

The approach used is based on the assessment of factors in the lives of your local children and what their risks are to succumbing to the above-mentioned undesirable outcomes. It also assesses what factors are already present in your community that can serve to help protect children from seeking to follow a path to the common problems of our youth. It helps identify gaps in providing the choice of a better path to follow and provides research-proven options to help fill those gaps.

Originally, this was a program for which your community would pay for the instruction and assistance. The step-by-step information has been purchased by SAMHSA and is available for your community to use free of charge.

A program like this is maximally effective only if you have the sustained cooperation and coordination of multiple community partners. The Community Anti-Drug Coalitions of America (CADCA) did an excellent job assessing the factors necessary for sustaining a coalition. You can find that information by going to cadca.org/CoalitionResources/Funding.asp, where you'll find an article titled "Funding." You'll need to scroll down to the section titled "Coalition Sustainability." Please take the time to read and consider their thoughts.

Further explore Communities That Care at preventionplatform.samhsa.gov, or call 1-240-276-2577.

AdvancED

AdvancED has recently combined the work of regional accreditation and school improvement organizations, which have been in existence since 1895, with the National Study of School Evaluation (NSSE) that was founded in 1933 by the six regional school accreditation commissions in the United

States. The NSSE's work on the *Cooperative Study of Secondary School Standards* was noted multiple times within this book and I believe was well represented by the philosophy expressed at the beginning of chapter 4.

The school improvement process that was the focus of the original study was based on: what the characteristics of a good school are, how you evaluate a school's effectiveness in relation to its objectives, how a good school becomes better, and how to stimulate schools to continue to strive to become better. These questions continue to be at the forefront of the work of the NSSE as it serves as the research and development arm of AdvancED.

AdvancED exists to advance excellence in education by providing products and services geared toward continuous improvement based on research and best practices, with student learning being the focus. The accreditation process they offer is voluntary with three criteria on which accreditation is made: (1) the schools must meet seven standards for quality, (2) the schools must be continuously improving, and (3) the schools must use an ongoing process of self-assessment in addition to outside review every five years.

You should not groan about the seven standards; I assure you these are not like your long list of state standards. These standards instruct schools that they must: have a clear vision and purpose, effective leadership, and a rigorous curriculum that's taught using research-based methods, use performance tools and indicate the results, have adequate resources and support for their programs, and demonstrate how they value stakeholders and communicate with them effectively.

Visit their website at www.advanc-ed.org to read further about their standards for schools and districts. You'll also find a section for parents and the public.

Parent and Community Participation

PTO Today

PTO Today is a private company that is serving as a valuable resource for parent groups including both PTAs and PTOs. If you are not familiar with the difference between those two organizations, you may want to start by looking at an article available at www.ptotoday.com that explains the difference. The PTO Today website is full of information, including many free articles, and also serves parent group marketers.

PTO Today also publishes the *PTO Today* magazine six times a year and the *Jump In!* magazine yearly during back-to-school season. PTO Today is the property of School Family Media, the focus of which is to enable and promote parental involvement in schools.

National Parent Teacher Association (PTA)

The national PTA was founded as a volunteer organization in 1897 with the vision of creating an organization centered on the idea of making children's lives better. All these years later and they have maintained that idea as their goal by providing a network of support and timely information on a variety of issues related to the health and education of children. Their current vision is to make "every child's potential a reality."

Working toward their continually challenging goal, the PTA serves many purposes including addressing legislative issues and promoting collaborative efforts between parents, teachers, and the greater community including the spiritual community. They recognize a family's spirituality as important while also recognizing that this is a pluralistic society. This nonprofit organization welcomes all. You do not have to be a parent or teacher to join. If you want to volunteer to help the children in your area but aren't comfortable working in the classrooms, this would be a good option to consider.

Having worked with busy parents for many years, if other people are willing to step up and head a local chapter, you'll find parents thankful and ready to help. Minimal dues exist for all members and there is a fee to start a new chapter. You may want to consider looking for a sponsor for that fee and many district administrations have served as such a sponsor. Joining is easy and you have the freedom to design your program to fit your needs. You can view their website at www.pta.org or call 1-800-307-4782 for more information.

Parent Networks

Parent Networks targets the preadolescent and teen years by building a community support network of parents with the goal of providing a unified effort in creating the expectations of safe and healthy choices. This networking began through the efforts of the mayor of Anchorage, Alaska, in 1995.

The idea seems to have been based on the common assumption that, with the expansion of your children's friends and associations within large schools and communities, parents are finding it difficult to know who their children's friends are, let alone have contact with the friends' parents. This has lead to the breakdown of the once common and effective principle that parents know "the who, what, and where" of their children's activities.

An easy-to-read two-page outline called "Creating a Successful Parent Network" can be found at www.preventionnetwork.org. Other websites are available and I would also recommend you check with your Cooperative Extension System to see if it is a program that they have acquired.

In my state, they have put together a very nice packet that includes a one-page "Steps to Building a Parent Network in Your Community" and a sturdy "Get Connected" telephone list for you to use. That's really all you need to get started. It appears simple and inexpensive, and the claim has been that it has helped make kids safer and decreased crime.

Schools That Make a Difference

National Community Education Association (NCEA)
The NCEA is a nonprofit organization devoted to the idea of creating opportunities for community members to be partners in addressing the needs of their own community of learners. They strive to accomplish this through a community education director who works to help identify the community's needs and resources. Based on the needs and resources, the education facilities offer a wide variety of youth and adult programs and activities. They look to their directors to facilitate cooperation and collaboration.

The principles that they follow to effectively establish the community education idea are that we should share the responsibility to provide lifelong learning opportunities to all ages, the people themselves should be involved in determining their own needs and identifying their resources, people become part of the solution when they develop the capacity to help themselves, local leadership development is essential, the efficient use of existing public institutions and services must be cooperatively utilized, and the services must be located for easy use by the public.

This information and more can be accessed at www.ncea.com.

Coalition of Essential Schools

The Coalition of Essential Schools (CES) is an organization founded by Ted Sizer in 1984 and is based on the idea that school reform is a local issue that is solved by people working together to develop a shared vision that becomes reality through their own community's strengths.

Therefore, each school is different but they all share the common principles upon which the coalition was established. Those principles include schooling based on the individual's needs and interests, creation of a climate of trust and high expectations, the establishment of student assessments based on performance and done in multiple ways, the development of close community ties that result in "real-world" learning opportunities, and the modeling of democratic practices.

Those that have followed the beliefs of CES have developed schools that have avoided the pitfalls of the standards movement; that does not mean they don't have their own high standards of performance for their students—they do. However, it does make it difficult to compare CES schools to the more traditional public schools. With a little investigating, you should be able to follow the trail and make your own conclusions by starting first at www.essentialschools.org or phoning 1-510-433-1451.

Additional Sources of Information

The Internet

Once again, I caution you to consider your source. If you are looking to compare school assessments, the number of organizations evaluating educational statistics has multiplied as fast as the number of tests themselves. And I would ask you to consider how relevant you believe the tests to be and who sponsors the site, and question their motivation. Ask questions and evaluate critically.

Your Own State Departments or Boards of Education

Each state has information on its own schools' assessment statistics and a variety of programs and other information. I would recommend that, if you have general questions or aren't sure who to contact, you call the U.S. Department of Education (listed below), and they may be able to answer your questions or know who to direct you to in your given state.

U.S. Department of Education

The U.S. Department of Education has a wealth of information that you may very well find overwhelming. Currently, some of their assessment summaries are not written as clearly as they could be, but, when you have a specific item you are searching for, the numbers themselves should be reliable. They do not currently provide any ranking of the states.

On December 5, 2008, as I was working on completion of this section, I phoned the U.S. Department of Education to explore what advice they would have to offer a citizen wanting to help improve schools. 1-800-872-5327 is the number for the Education Information Resource Center, but, as my luck would have it, instead of a person, I got a recording that they were temporarily "offline." The recording referred callers to answers.ed.gov or www.ed.gov. Later, the live service was once again available, and, as in the past, the person answering was helpful, knowledgeable, and very cordial.

That was a truly fortunate series of events; I may have neglected to make a very important point. Websites are great if you have access, but it isn't right to expect that everyone has Internet service in their homes. As requirements for life, it seems that, along with food, water, shelter, and I would add clean air, we now consider the Internet as essential.

Many organizations, not just the government, depend too heavily on written material to get information into the minds of those that can make use of it. Just because someone can't read or doesn't have access to information should not put them into the category of a useless, worthless human being. An illiterate person may not be able to help teach children to read but that doesn't mean they don't have time to donate or some character traits or a talent that is worthy of our attention and that could contribute to school improvement. That doesn't mean that they aren't hard-working and willing to help. They shouldn't be marginalized from participating in the education system of a democratic society because of our shortsightedness or lack of understanding. These overlooked human resources are probably the very same parents, grandparents, and citizens that we badly need to draw into an improvement process. That won't happen when they immediately encounter a barrier to their participation.

If a person truly cares about the education of children, their voice should unconditionally be heard.

ABOUT THE AUTHOR

Victoria M. Young earned both her bachelor of science in animal husbandry and doctorate of veterinary medicine from Michigan State University, and is a member of the Idaho Writers Guild. Her two children were born in Brookings, South Dakota. Both are high school graduates, currently attending college, and do make her very proud when they enjoy reading a good book for entertainment.

She was able to balance her career around the desire to be home with her children and to serve in her children's classrooms. Those efforts were acknowledged with a Friend of Caldwell Schools Award in recognition of support for education and the pursuit of excellence. She currently resides in Caldwell, Idaho, with her husband, two dogs, and two cats. She frequently visits her home state of Michigan and enjoys floating the river nature provided in her old stomping grounds.